POEMS
IN FOCUS

Christopher Martin

Oxford University Press

Oxford University Press, Walton Street, Oxford OX2 6DP

Oxford New York Toronto
Delhi Bombay Calcutta Madras Karachi
Petaling Jaya Singapore Hong Kong Tokyo
Nairobi Dar es Salaam Cape Town
Melbourne Auckland

and associated companies in
Beirut Berlin Ibadan Nicosia

Oxford is a trade mark of Oxford University Press

ISBN 0 19 831248 2

Typeset by Keyspools Ltd, Golborne, Lancs
Printed in Great Britain at the University Press, Cambridge

CONTENTS

WAR

The First World War

The Second World War

After World War II

THE NATURAL WORLD

Man and Nature

The Seasons

LOVE AND MARRIAGE

Love

Marriage

PEOPLE

Children and Parents

6

REFLECTIONS AND IMAGININGS

Reflections

Imaginings

COME ALONG, BOYS!

"The moment the order came to go forward, there were smiling faces everywhere."
(Extract from letter written in the trenches of the Aisne by General Sir Horace Smith-Dorrien).

ENLIST TO-DAY

THE HAYCOCK-CADLE CO., LONDON, S.E.

Published by the Parliamentary Recruiting Committee, London. Poster No. 22.

WAR

THE FIRST WORLD WAR

He went for a Soldier

He marched away with a blithe* young score of him   carefree and light-
    With the first volunteers,   hearted
Clear-eyed and clean and sound to the core of him,
    Blushing under the cheers.
They were fine, new flags that swung a-flying there,
Oh, the pretty girls he glimpsed a-crying there,
    Pelting him with pinks and with roses –
    Billy, the Soldier Boy!

Not very clear in the kind young heart of him
    What the fuss was about,
But the flowers and the flags seemed part of him –
    The music drowned his doubt.
It's a fine, brave sight they were a-coming there
To the gay, bold tune they kept a-drumming there,
    While the boasting fifes shrilled jauntily –
    Billy, the Soldier Boy!

Soon he is one with the blinding smoke of it –
    Volley and curse and groan:
Then he has done with the knightly joke of it –
    It's rending flesh and bone.
There are pain-crazed animals a-shrieking there
And a warm blood stench that is a-reeking there;
    He fights like a rat in a corner –
    Billy, the Soldier Boy!

There he lies now, like a ghoulish score of him,
    Left on the field for dead:
The ground all around is smeared with the gore* of him –   blood
    Even the leaves are red.
The Thing that was Billy lies a-dying there,
Writhing and a-twisting and a-crying there;
    A sickening sun grins down on him –
    Billy, the Soldier Boy!

Still not quite clear in the poor, wrung heart of him
　　What the fuss was about,
See where he lies – or a ghastly part of him –
　　While life is oozing out:
There are loathsome things he sees a-crawling there;
There are hoarse-voiced crows he hears a-calling there,
　　Eager for the foul feast spread for them –
　　Billy, the Soldier Boy!

Ruth Comfort Mitchell

The Volunteer

Here lies a clerk who half his life had spent
Toiling at ledgers* in a city grey,   account books
Thinking that so his days would drift away
With no lance broken in life's tournament.
Yet ever 'twixt the books and his bright eyes
The gleaming eagles of the legions came,
And horsemen, charging under phantom skies,
Went thundering past beneath the oriflamme*.   banner

And now those waiting dreams are satisfied;
From twilight to the halls of dawn he went;
His lance is broken; but he lies content
With that high hour, in which he lived and died.
And falling thus he wants no recompense,
Who found his battle in the last resort;
Nor needs he any hearse to bear him hence,   a famous battle against
Who goes to join the men of Agincourt*.   the French won by
                                                                         King Henry V in 1415

Herbert Asquith

Buttons

I have been watching the war map slammed up for
    advertising in front of the newspaper office.
Buttons – red and yellow buttons – blue and black buttons
    – are shoved back and forth across the map.

A laughing young man, sunny with freckles,
Climbs a ladder, yells a joke to somebody in the crowd,
And then fixes a yellow button one inch west
And follows the yellow button with a black button one inch
    west.

(Ten thousand men and boys twist on their bodies in a red
    soak along a river edge,
Gasping of wounds, calling for water, some rattling death in
    their throats.)
Who would guess what it cost to move two buttons one inch
    on the war map here in front of the newspaper office
    where the freckle-faced young man is laughing to us?

Carl Sandburg

The Night Patrol

'Over the top! The wire's* thin here, unbarbed   barbed wire
Plain rusty coils, not staked, and low enough:
Full of old tins, though – When you're through, all three,
Aim quarter left for fifty yards or so,
Then straight for that new piece of German wire;
See if it's thick, and listen for a while
For sounds of working; don't run any risks;
About an hour; now, over!'

                              And we placed
Our hands on the topmost sand-bags, leapt, and stood
A second with curved backs, then crept to the wire,
Wormed ourselves tinkling through, glanced back, and
      dropped.
The sodden ground was splashed with shallow pools,
And tufts of crackling cornstalks, two years old,
No man had reaped, and patches of spring grass,
Half-seen, as rose and sank the flares, were strewn
With the wreck of our attack: the bandoliers*,   cartridge belts
Packs, rifles, bayonets, belts, and haversacks,
Shell fragments, and the huge whole forms of shells
Shot fruitlessly – and everywhere the dead.
Only the dead were always present – present
As a vile sickly smell of rottenness;
The rustling stubble and the early grass,
The slimy pools – the dead men stank through all,
Pungent and sharp; as bodies loomed before,
And as we passed, they stank; then dulled away
To that vague foetor*, all encompassing,   stink
Infecting earth and air. They lay, all clothed,
Each in some new and piteous attitude
That we well marked to guide us back; as* he,   like
Outside our wire, that lay on his back and crossed
His legs Crusader-wise*; I smiled at that,   like a knight's statue on
And thought of Elia* and his Temple Church.   a tomb
From him, a quarter left, lay a small corpse,   Charles Lamb, the 19th
Down in a hollow, huddled as in bed,   century essay writer
That one of us put his hand on unawares.
Next was a bunch of half a dozen men
All blown to bits, an archipelago*   like a group of islands
Of corrupt fragments, vexing to us three,
Who had no light to see by, save the flares.
On such a trail, so lit, for ninety yards
We crawled on belly and elbows, till we saw,
Instead of lumpish dead before our eyes,
The stakes and crosslines of the German wire.
We lay in shelter of the last dead man,
Ourselves as dead, and heard their* shovels ring   German
Turning the earth, their talk and cough at times.

A sentry fired and a machine-gun spat;
They shot a flare above us; when it fell
And spluttered out in the pools of No Man's Land,
We turned and crawled past the remembered dead;
Past him and him, and them and him, until,
For he lay some way apart, we caught the scent
Of the Crusader and slid past his legs,
And through the wire and home, and got our rum.

Arthur Graeme West

The Hero

'Jack fell as he'd have wished,' the Mother said,
And folded up the letter that she'd read.
'The Colonel writes so nicely.' Something broke
In the tired voice that quavered to a choke.
She half looked up. 'We mothers are so proud
Of our dead soldiers.' Then her face was bowed.

Quietly the Brother Officer went out.
He'd told the poor old dear some gallant lies
That she would nourish all her days, no doubt.
For while he coughed and mumbled, her weak eyes
Had shone with gentle triumph, brimmed with joy,
Because he'd been so brave, her glorious boy.

He thought how 'Jack', cold-footed, useless swine,
Had panicked down the trench that night the mine
Went up at Wicked Corner*; how he'd tried   part of a trench system
To get sent home, and how, at last, he died,
Blown to small bits. And no one seemed to care
Except that lonely woman with white hair.

Siegfried Sassoon

Suicide in the Trenches

I knew a simple soldier boy
Who grinned at life in empty joy,
Slept soundly through the lonesome dark,
And whistled early with the lark.

In winter trenches, cowed and glum,
With crumps* and lice and lack of rum,   explosions
He put a bullet through his brain.
No one spoke of him again.

           *   *   *

You smug-faced crowds with kindling eye*   gleaming with
Who cheer when soldier lads march by,   enthusiasm for war
Sneak home and pray you'll never know
The hell where youth and laughter go.

Siegfried Sassoon

The Effect

'The effect of our bombardment was terrific. One man told
    me he had never seen so many dead before.' *War*
    correspondent

'He'd never seen so many dead before.'
They sprawled in yellow daylight while he swore
And gasped and lugged his everlasting load
Of bombs along what once had been a road.
'How peaceful are the dead.'
Who put that silly gag* in some one's head?   catch-phrase

'He'd never seen so many dead before.'
The lilting words danced up and down his brain,
While corpses jumped and capered in the rain.
No, no; he wouldn't count them any more . . .
The dead have done with pain:
They've choked; they can't come back to life again.

When Dick was killed last week he looked like that,
Flapping along the fire-step like a fish,
After the blazing crump* had knocked him flat . . .   shell explosion
'How many dead? As many as ever you wish.
Don't count 'em; they're too many.
Who'll buy my nice fresh corpses, two a penny?'

Siegfried Sassoon

Great Men

The great ones of the earth
Approve, with smiles and bland salutes, the rage
And monstrous tyranny* they have brought to birth.   cruel exercise of power
The great ones of the earth
Are much concerned about the wars they wage,
And quite aware of what those wars are worth.

         *   *   *

You Marshals, gilt and red,
You Ministers and Princes, and Great Men,
Why can't you keep your mouthings for the dead?
Go round the simple cemeteries; and then
Talk of our noble sacrifice and losses
To the wooden crosses.

Siegfried Sassoon

The Target

I shot him, and it had to be
One of us! 'Twas him or me.
'Couldn't be helped,' and none can blame
Me, for you would do the same.

My mother, she can't sleep for fear
Of what might be a-happening here
To me. Perhaps it might be best
To die, and set her fears at rest.

For worst is worst, and worry's done.
Perhaps he was the only son . . .
Yet God keeps still, and does not say
A word of guidance any way.

Well, if they get* me, first I'll find   kill
That boy, and tell him all my mind,
And see who felt the bullet worst,
And ask his pardon, if I durst*.   dare

All's a tangle. Here's my job.
A man might rave, or shout, or sob;
And God He takes no sort of heed.
This is a bloody mess indeed.

Ivor Gurney

Not to keep

They sent him back to her. The letter came
Saying . . . And she could have him. And before
She could be sure there was no hidden ill
Under the formal writing, he was there,
Living. They gave him back to her alive –
How else? They are not known to send the dead –
And not disfigured visibly. His face?
His hands? She had to look, to look and ask,
'What is it, dear?' And she had given all
And still she had all – *they* had – they the lucky!
Wasn't she glad now? Everything seemed won,
And all the rest for them permissible* ease.   allowable
She had to ask, 'What was it, dear?'

                                        'Enough,
Yet not enough. A bullet through and through,
High in the breast. Nothing but what good care
And medicine and rest, and you a week,
Can cure me of to go again.' The same
Grim giving to do over for them both.
She dared no more than ask him with her eyes
How was it with him for a second trial.
And with his eyes he asked her not to ask.
They had given him back to her, but not to keep.

Robert Frost

Spring Offensive

Halted against the shade of a last hill
They fed, and eased of pack-loads, were at ease;
And leaning on the nearest chests or knees
Carelessly slept.
             But many there stood still
To face the stark blank sky beyond the ridge,
Knowing their feet had come to the end of the world.
Marvelling they stood, and watched the long grass swirled
By the May breeze, murmurous with wasp and midge;
And though the summer oozed into their veins
Like an injected drug for their bodies' pains,
Sharp on their souls hung the imminent ridge of grass*,   the skyline they are
                                                               about to cross
Fearfully flashed the sky's mysterious glass.

Hour after hour they ponder the warm field
And the far valley behind, where buttercups
Had blessed with gold their slow boots coming up;
When even the little brambles would not yield
But clutched and clung to them like sorrowing arms.
They breathe like trees unstirred.

Till like a cold gust thrills the little word
At which each body and its soul begird*   get ready
And tighten them for battle. No alarms
Of bugles, no high flags, no clamorous haste, –
Only a lift and flare of eyes that faced
The sun, like a friend with whom their love is done.
O larger shone that smile against the sun, –
Mightier than his* whose bounty* these have spurned.   God's gifts

So, soon they topped the hill, and raced together
Over an open stretch of herb and heather
Exposed. And instantly the whole sky burned
With fury against them; earth set sudden cups
In thousands for their blood; and the green slope
Chasmed* and deepened sheer to infinite space.   became a deep gulf

Of them who running on that last high place
Breasted the surf of bullets, or went up
On the hot blast and fury of hell's upsurge,
Or plunged and fell away past this world's verge,
Some say God caught them even before they fell.

But what say such as from existence' brink
Ventured but drave too swift to sink,
The few who rushed in the body to enter hell,
And there out-fiending all its fiends and flames
With superhuman inhumanities,
Long-famous glories, immemorial* shames –   ancient
And crawling slowly back, have by degrees
Regained cool peaceful air in wonder –
Why speak not they of comrades that went under?

Wilfred Owen

The Send-Off

Down the close darkening lanes they sang their way
To the siding-shed,
And lined the train with faces grimly gay.

Their breasts were stuck all white with wreath and spray
As men's are, dead.

Dull porters watched them, and a casual tramp
Stood staring hard,
Sorry to miss them from the upland camp.

Then, unmoved, signals nodded, and a lamp
Winked to the guard.

So secretly, like wrongs, hushed-up, they went.
They were not ours:
We never heard to which front these were sent;

Nor there if they yet mock what women meant
Who gave them flowers.

Shall they return to beating of great bells
In wild train-loads?
A few, a few, too few for drums and yells,

May creep back, silent, to village wells,
Up half-known roads.

Wilfred Owen

Futility

Move him into the sun –
Gently its touch awoke him once,
At home, whispering of fields half-sown.
Always it woke him, even in France,
Until this morning and this snow.
If anything might rouse him now
The kind old sun will know.

Think how it wakes the seeds –
Woke once the clays of a cold star.
Are limbs, so dear achieved, are side
Full-nerved, still warm, too hard to stir?
Was it for this the clay* grew tall?
– O what made fatuous* sunbeams toil
To break earth's sleep at all?

Wilfred Owen

according to Biblical
story, man was created
from clay

purposeless

The Armistice*

end of fighting in a war

The news came through over the telephone:
All the terms had been signed: the War was won:
And all the fighting and the agony,
And all the labour of the years were done.
One girl clicked sudden at her typewriter
And whispered, 'Jerry's safe,' and sat and stared:
One said, 'It's over, over, it's the end:
The War is over: ended': and a third,
'I can't remember life without the war'.
And one came in and said, 'Look here, they say
We can all go at five to celebrate,
As long as two stay on, just for today'.

It was quite quiet in the big empty room
Among the typewriters and little piles
Of index cards: one said, 'We'd better just
Finish the day's reports and do the files'.
And said, 'It's awf'lly like *Recessional*,   a famous poem by
Now when the tumult has all died away'.   Rudyard Kipling
The other said, 'Thank God we saw it through;
I wonder what they'll do at home today'.
And said, 'You know it will be quiet tonight
Up at the Front: first time in all these years,
And no one will be killed there any more',
And stopped, to hide her tears.
She said, 'I've told you; he was killed in June'.
The other said, 'My dear, I know; I know . . .
It's over for me too . . . My man was killed,
Wounded . . . and died . . . at Ypres* . . . three years ago . . .   Belgian town
And he's my man, and I want him,' she said,
And knew that peace could not give back her dead.

May Wedderburn Cannan

The Son

I found the letter in a cardboard box,
Unfamous history. I read the words.
The ink was frail* and brown, the paper dry   faint
After so many years of being kept.
The letter was a soldier's, from the front –
Conveyed his love and disappointed hope
Of getting leave. 'It's cancelled now,' he wrote.
'My luck is at the bottom of the sea.'

Outside the sun was hot; the world looked bright;
I heard a radio, and someone laughed.
I did not sing, or laugh, or love the sun.
Within the quiet room I thought of him,
My father killed, and all the other men,
Whose luck was at the bottom of the sea.

Clifford Dyment

MCMXIV*   1914

Those long uneven lines
Standing as patiently
As if they were stretched outside
The Oval or Villa Park*,   famous cricket and
                                                             football grounds
The crowns of hats, the sun
On moustached archaic* faces   old-fashioned
Grinning as if it were all
An August Bank Holiday lark;

And the shut shops, the bleached
Established names on the sunblinds,

The farthings and sovereigns*,
And dark-clothed children at play
Called after kings and queens,
The tin advertisements
For cocoa and twist*, and the pubs
Wide open all day;

small and large value
coins

tobacco

And the countryside not caring:
The place-names all hazed over
With flowering grasses, and fields
Shadowing Domesday* lines
Under wheat's restless silence;
The differently-dressed servants
With tiny rooms in huge houses,
The dust behind limousines;

boundary lines
set down in the
land survey of
King William I

Never such innocence,
Never before or since,
As changed itself to past
Without a word – the men
Leaving the gardens tidy,
The thousands of marriages
Lasting a little while longer:
Never such innocence again.

Philip Larkin

War Blinded

For more than sixty years he has been blind
Behind that wall, these trees, with terrible
Longevity* wheeled in the sun and wind   long life
On pathways of the soldiers' hospital.

For half that time his story's troubled me –
That showroom by the ferry, where I saw
His basketwork, a touch-turned filigree*   delicate handwork
His fingers coaxed from charitable straw;

Or how he felt when young, enlisting at
Recruiting tables on the football pitch,
To end up slumped across a parapet*,   side of a trench
His eye-blood running in a molten ditch;

Or how the light looked when I saw two men,
One blind, one in a wheelchair, in that park,
Their dignity, which I have not forgotten,
Which helps me struggle with this lesser dark.

That war's too old for me to understand
How he might think, nursed now in wards of want,
Remembering that day when his right hand
Gripped on the shoulder of the man in front.

Douglas Dunn

THE SECOND WORLD WAR

Epitaph* on a Tyrant

inscription on a
tombstone

Perfection, of a kind, was what he was after,
And the poetry he invented was easy to understand;
He knew human folly like the back of his hand,
And was greatly interested in armies and fleets;
When he laughed, respectable senators* burst with
    laughter,
And when he cried the little children died in the streets.

members of
government

W. H. Auden

Refugee Blues

Say this city has ten million souls,
Some are living in mansions, some are living in holes:
Yet there's no place for us, my dear, yet there's no place for
    us.

Once we had a country and we thought it fair,
Look in the atlas and you'll find it there:
We cannot go there now, my dear, we cannot go there now.

In the village churchyard there grows an old yew,
Every spring it blossoms anew:
Old passports can't do that, my dear, old passports can't do
    that.

The consul banged the table and said:
'If you've no passport you're officially dead':
But we are still alive, my dear, but we are still alive.

Went to a committee; they offered me a chair;
Asked me politely to return next year:
But where shall we go today, my dear, but where shall we
    go today?

Came to a public meeting; the speaker got up and said:
'If we let them in, they will steal our daily bread';
He was talking of you and me, my dear, he was talking of
    you and me.

Thought I heard the thunder rumbling in the sky;
It was Hitler over Europe, saying: 'They must die';
We were in his mind, my dear, we were in his mind.

Saw a poodle in a jacket fastened with a pin,
Saw a door opened and a cat let in:
But they weren't German Jews, my dear, but they weren't
    German Jews.

Went down to the harbour and stood upon the quay,
Saw the fish swimming as if they were free:
Only ten feet away, my dear, only ten feet away.

Walked through a wood, saw the birds in the trees;
They had no politicians and sang at their ease:
They weren't the human race, my dear, they weren't the
    human race.

Dreamed I saw a building with a thousand floors,
A thousand windows and a thousand doors;
Not one of them was ours, my dear, not one of them was
    ours.

Stood on a great plain in the falling snow:
Ten thousand soldiers marched to and fro:
Looking for you and me, my dear, looking for you and me.

W. H. Auden

Embassy[*]

diplomat's office

As evening fell the day's oppression lifted;
Tall peaks came into focus; it had rained:
Across wide lawns and cultured* flowers drifted
The conversation of the highly trained.

carefully grown

Thin gardeners watched them pass and priced their shoes:
A chauffeur waited, reading in the drive,
For them to finish their exchange of views;
It looked a picture of the way to live.

Far off, no matter what good they intended,
Two armies waited for a verbal error
With well-made implements for causing pain:

And on the issue of their charm depended
A land laid waste with all its young men slain,
Its women weeeping, and its towns in terror.

W. H. Auden

Night Raid

The sleepers humped down on the benches,
The daft boy was playing rummy with anyone he could get,
And the dancing girl said, 'What I say is,
If there's a bomb made for YOU,
You're going to get it.'
Someone muttered, 'The bees are coming again.'
Someone whispered beside me in the darkness,
'They're coming up from the east.'
Way off the guns muttered distantly.

This was in the small hours, at the ebb.
And the dancing girl clicked her teeth like castanets
And said, 'I don't mind life, believe me.
I like it. If there is any more to come,
I can take it and be glad of it.'
She was shivering and laughing and throwing her head
    back.
On the pavement men looked up thoughtfully,
Making plausible* conjectures. The night sky
Throbbed under the cool bandage of the searchlights.

guesses that seemed reasonable

Desmond Hawkins

Days drawing in

The days fail: night broods over afternoon:
And at my child's first drink beyond the night
Her skin is silver in the early light.
Sweet the grey morning and the raiders gone.

E. J. Scovell

The Bombing of the Café de Paris, 1941

Snakehips, the bandleader, wore a gallant grin,
A clip of white cartridges; he and the boys
Tapped natty polished toes to keep the time
Of tango, quickstep, foxtrot, blues and swing;
The basement of the place was deep and safe,
No other-ranks or bombs would be let in.

A boy in Air force blue danced with his mother;
A sub-lieutenant stroked his girl's silk knee;
Caressing lights lay soft on hair and flesh,
Bright on badges, deep in polished leather.
A major of the Black Watch called for Scotch
And winked at his admiring younger brother.

Oh Johnny, Oh Johnny, how you can love,
That was the song they liked. They could forget
That loving wasn't all that he must do:
Oh Johnny, Oh Johnny, heavens above –
And in the hidden heavens the siren's wailing
Mourned over London and the shattered dove.

But no one there could hear. The music gushed
And wine corks popped like children's wooden guns.
No warning when the bomb came bursting in,
Huge knuckle-dustered fist that struck and crushed
Furniture of wood and flesh; the bang's
Enormous shadow paled; the place was hushed.

Some light remained, and from the ceiling came
Floating down a fine cosmetic dust
That settled softly on the hair and skin
Of the sailor's girl, who, wholly without shame,
Sprawled in ripped clothes, one precious stocking gone
And with it half her leg. No one would blame

Her carelessness for once, and if they did
She would not care. The sailor lay beneath
Dark flood of fallen curtain, quiet and still,
As if he rested on the ocean bed.
The airman's mother sat upon the floor,
Crooned comfort to her child's deaf cradled head.

Snakehips had put away his grin forever.
Music might return, but he would not.
The kilted major found another drink
Then carried out his brother, like an order,
Joining the stunned survivors in the street,
Sick from their meeting with the dark marauder*.   attacker

While, down below, a woman lay and saw
A man approaching through the powdery gloom;
She could not move trapped limbs. 'Rescue!' she thought
As by her side he knelt upon the floor,
Reached out to finger at her neck and take
Her string of pearls in one triumphant paw.

Outside, the sirens once again composed
A mocking dirge above the crouching town;
Along the blackened streets on nervous wheels
The blinkered ambulances gently nosed,
Ferrying cool instruments of mercy.
An incident of war was almost closed.

Vernon Scannell

The Evacuee

She woke up under a loose quilt
Of leaf patterns, woven by the light
At the small window, busy with the boughs
Of a young cherry; but wearily she lay,
Waiting for the siren*, slow to trust   air-raid warning
Nature's deceptive peace, and then afraid
Of the long silence, she would have crept
Uneasily from the bedroom with its frieze*   band of sunlight on a
Of fresh sunlight, had not a cock crowed,   wall
Shattering the surface of that limpid* pool   clear
Of stillness, and before the ripples died
One by one in the field's shallows,
The farm woke with uninhibited* din.   unrestrained

And now the noise and not the silence drew her
Down the bare stairs at great speed.
The sounds and voices were a rough sheet
Waiting to catch her, as though she leaped
From a scorched storey* of the charred past.   burning building

And there the table and the gallery
Of farm faces trying to be kind
Beckoned her nearer, and she sat down
Under an awning* of salt hams.

protective shelter

And so she grew, a small bird in the nest
Of welcome that was built about her,
Home now after so long away
In the flowerless streets of the drab town.
The men watched her busy with the hens,
The soft flesh ripening warm as corn
On the sticks of limbs, the grey eyes clear,
Rinsed with dew of their long dread.
The men watched her, and, nodding, smiled
With earth's charity, patient and strong.

R. S. Thomas

Vergissmeinnicht*

don't forget me

Three weeks gone and the combatants gone
returning over the nightmare ground
we found the place again, and found
the soldier sprawling in the sun.

The frowning barrel of his gun
overshadowing. As we came on
that day, he hit my tank with one
like the entry of a demon.

Look. Here in the gunpit spoil
the dishonoured picture of his girl
who has put: *Steffi*. *Vergissmeinnicht*
in a copybook gothic* script.

Steve

German writing

We see him almost with content,
abased, and seeming to have paid
and mocked at by his own equipment
that's hard and good when he's decayed.

But she would weep to see today
how on his skin the swart* flies move;   dark
the dust upon the paper eye
and the burst stomach like a cave.

For here the lover and killer are mingled
who had one body and one heart.
And death who had the soldier singled*   selected
has done the lover mortal* hurt.   fatal

Keith Douglas

The Battle

Helmet and rifle, pack and overcoat
Marched through a forest. Somewhere up ahead
Guns thudded. Like the circle of a throat
The night on every side was turning red.

They halted and they dug. They sank like moles
Into the clammy earth between the trees.
And soon the sentries, standing in their holes,
Felt the first snow. Their feet began to freeze.

At dawn the first shell landed with a crack.
Then shells and bullets swept the icy woods.
This lasted many days. The snow was black.
The corpses stiffened in their scarlet hoods.

Most clearly of that battle I remember
The tiredness in eyes, how hands looked thin
Around a cigarette, and the bright ember
Would pulse with all the life there was within.

Louis Simpson

A Front[*]

meaning both bad
weather and the
frontline of battle

Fog over the base: the beams ranging
From the five towers pull home from the night
The crews cold in fur, the bombers banging
Like lost trucks down the levels of the ice.
A glow drifts in like mist (how many tons of it?),
Bounces to a roll, turns suddenly to steel
And tyres and turrets, huge in the trembling light.
The next is high, and pulls up with a wail,
Comes round again – no use. And no use for the rest
In drifting circles out along the range;
Holding no longer, changed to a kinder course,
The flights drone southward through the steady rain.
The base is closed . . . But one voice keeps on calling,
The lowering pattern of the engines grows;
The roar gropes downward in its shaky orbit
For the lives the season quenches. Here below
They beg, order, are not heard; and hear the darker
Voice rising: Can't you hear me? Over. Over –
All the air quivers, and the east sky glows.

Randall Jarrell

The Interrogation

We could have crossed the road but hesitated,
And then came the patrol;
The leader conscientious and intent,
The men surly, indifferent.
While we stood by and waited
The interrogation began. He says the whole
Must come out now, who, what we are,
Where we have come from, with what purpose, whose
Country or camp we plot for or betray.
Question on question.

We have stood and answered through the standing day
And watched across the road beyond the hedge
The careless lovers in pairs go by,
Hand linked in hand, wandering another star,
So near we could shout to them. We cannot choose
Answer or action here,
Though still the careless lovers saunter by
And the thoughtless field is near.
We are on the very edge,
Endurance almost done,
And still the interrogation is going on.

Edwin Muir

Anne Frank Huis*

Anne Frank's house in Amsterdam, Holland

Even now, after twice her lifetime of grief
and anger in the very place, whoever comes
to climb these narrow stairs, discovers how
the bookcase slides aside, then walks through
shadow into sunlit rooms, can never help

but break her secrecy again. Just listening
is a kind of guilt: the Westerkerk* repeats

a nearby church clock

itself outside, as if all time worked round
towards her fear, and made each stroke die
down on guarded streets. Imagine it –

three years of ·whispering and loneliness
and plotting, day by day, the Allied line
in Europe with a yellow chalk. What hope
she had for ordinary love and interest
survives her here, displayed above the bed

as pictures of her family; some actors;
fashions chosen by Princess Elizabeth*.

later Queen Elizabeth II
of Britain

And those who stoop to see them find
not only patience missing its reward,
but one enduring wish for chances like

my own: to leave as simply as I do,
and walk where couples stroll at ease
up dusty tree-lined avenues, or watch
a silent barge come clear of bridges
settling their reflections in the blue canal.

Andrew Motion

War Cemetery, Ranville*

near Caen, in
Normandy, France

A still parade of stone tablets,
White as aspirin under the bland
Wash of an August sky, they stand
In exact battalions, their shoulders square.

I move slowly along the lines
Like a visiting Commander
Noting each rank, name and number
And that a few are without names.

All have been efficiently drilled,
They do not blink or shift beneath
My inspection; they do not breathe
Or sway in the hot summer air.

The warmth is sick with too much scent
And thick as ointment. Flowers hurt,
Their sweetness fed by dirt,
Breathing in the dark earth underneath.

Outside the cemetery walls
The children play; their shouts are thrown
High in the air, burst and come down
In shrapnel* softer than summer rain.

shell fragments

Vernon Scannell

AFTER WORLD WAR II

At the Bomb Testing Site

At noon in the desert a panting lizard
waited for history, its elbows tense,
watching the curve of a particular road
as if something might happen.

It was looking at something farther off
than people could see, an important scene
acted in stone for little selves
at the flute* end of consequences.   narrow channel

There was just a continent without much on it
under a sky that never cared less.
Ready for a change, the elbows waited,
the hands gripped hard on the desert.

William Stafford

Your Attention Please

The Polar DEW* has just warned that   Direct Early Warning
A nuclear rocket strike of   radar station
At least one thousand megatons*   Explosive force of
Has been launched by the enemy   1,000,000 tons of TNT
Directly at our major cities.
This announcement will take
Two and a quarter minutes to make,
You therefore have a further
Eight and a quarter minutes
To comply with the shelter
Requirements published in the Civil
Defence Code – section Atomic Attack.

A specially shortened Mass
Will be broadcast at the end
Of this announcement –
Protestant and Jewish Services
Will begin simultaneously –
Select your wavelength immediately
According to instructions
In the Defence Code. Do not
Take well-loved pets (including birds)
Into your shelter – they will consume
Fresh air. Leave the old and bed-
Ridden, you can do nothing for them.
Remember to press the sealing
Switch when everyone is in
The shelter. Set the radiation
Aerial, turn on the geiger barometer*.   device for detecting
Turn off your Television now.   radio-activity
Turn off your radio immediately
The Services end. At the same time
Secure explosion plugs in the ears
Of each member of your family. Take
Down your plasma* flasks. Give your children   blood for transfusion
The pills marked one and two
In the C.D. green container, then put
Them to bed. Do not break
The inside airlock seals until
The radiation All Clear shows
(Watch for the cuckoo in your
Perspex panel), or your District
Touring Doctor rings your bell.
If before this your air becomes
Exhausted or if any of your family
Is critically injured, administer
The capsules marked 'Valley Forge'*   American government
(Red pocket in No. 1 Survival Kit)   Defence suppliers
For painless death. (Catholics
Will have been instructed by their priests
What to do in this eventuality.)
This announcement is ending. Our President
Has already given orders for

Massive retaliation – it will be
Decisive. Some of us may die.
Remember, statistically
It is not likely to be you.
All flags are flying fully dressed
On Government buildings – the sun is shining.
Death is the least we have to fear.
We are all in the hands of God,
Whatever happens happens by His Will.
Now go quickly to your shelters.

Peter Porter

Home-Coming

All day, day after day, they're bringing them home*,   to Australia
they're picking them up, those they can find, and bringing
    them home,
they're bringing them in, piled on the hulls of Grants*, in   tanks
    trucks, in convoys,
they're zipping them up in green plastic bags,
they're tagging them now in Saigon*, in the mortuary   capital of South Vietnam
    coolness
they're giving them names, they're rolling them out of
the deep-freeze lockers – on the tarmac at Tan Son Nhut*   base in Vietnam
the noble jets are whining like hounds,
they are bringing them home
– curly-heads, kinky-hairs, crew-cuts, balding non-coms
– they're high, now, high and higher, over the land, the
steaming *chow mein*,   Chinese rice dish
their shadows are tracing the blue curve of the Pacific
with sorrowful quick fingers, heading south, heading east,
home, home, home – and the coasts swing upwards, the old
    ridiculous curvatures
of earth, the knuckled hills, the mangrove swamps, the
    desert emptiness . . .

in their sterile housing they tilt towards these like skiers
– taxiing in, on the long runways, the howl of their home-
    coming rises
surrounding them like their last moments (the mash, the
    splendour)
then fading at length as they move
on to small towns where dogs in the frozen sunset
raise muzzle in mute salute,
and on to cities in whose wide web of suburbs
telegrams tremble like leaves from a wintering tree
and the spider grief swings in his bitter geometry
– they're bringing them home, now, too late, too early.

Bruce Dawe

What were they like?

1) Did the people of Vietnam
    use lanterns of stone?
2) Did they hold ceremonies
    to reverence the opening of buds?
3) Were they inclined to quiet laughter?
4) Did they use bone and ivory,
    jade* and silver, for ornament?   green hard stone
5) Had they an epic poem?*   traditional story of
6) Did they distinguish between speech and singing? heroes

1) Sir, their light hearts turned to stone.
    It is not remembered whether in gardens
    stone lanterns illumined* pleasant ways.   lit up
2) Perhaps they gathered once to delight in blossom,
    but after the children were killed
    there were no more buds.
3) Sir, laughter is bitter to the burned mouth.
4) A dream ago, perhaps. Ornament is for joy.
    All the bones were charred.

5) It is not remembered. Remember,
   most were peasants; their life
   was in rice and bamboo.
   When peaceful clouds were reflected in the paddies*   rice fields
   and the water buffalo stepped surely along terraces,
   maybe fathers told their sons old tales.
   When bombs smashed those mirrors
   there was time only to scream.

6) There is an echo yet
   of their speech which was like a song.
   It was reported their singing resembled
   the flight of moths in moonlight.
   Who can say? It is silent now.

Denise Levertov

NOTES AND
SUGGESTIONS FOR WORK

▷: Topic for imaginative writing arising from ideas in the poem.

THE FIRST WORLD WAR

He went for a Soldier   *Ruth Comfort Mitchell*   10

Ruth Mitchell was an American poet who imagined, as an outsider, the horror of the war in Europe (America did not enter the fighting until 1917).

Billy is a typical young volunteer, caught up in the excitement of the war's opening. Which details in the first two verses make war seem attractive and colourful? What is admirable about Billy? What is sad about his knowledge of the war?

Which word in verse three reminds you of Asquith's *Volunteer*? What is the poet's opinion of that attitude to war? Which ugly words and ideas in the last three verses convey her disgust at war? Which of these hideous details do you find most forceful?

What is the effect of the refrain, *Billy, the Soldier Boy*, as the poem progresses?

The Volunteer   *Herbert Asquith*   11

Herbert Asquith, the younger son of H. H. Asquith (British Prime Minister 1908–1916), served in the war as an officer, and was wounded.

The clerk is a day-dreamer, who longs for the adventure of war as he works at his tedious job.

The first verse contrasts dreary reality and romantic dream. Which words and phrases describe the clerk's life? Which catch the colour and excitement of his vision of war?

The second verse describes the change in the clerk's life when war comes in 1914. What happens to him? How might he have felt about his fate? What does the poet think about him? Why does the poet use so many old-fashioned words?

Contrast the attitude to war in this poem with that in later poems of this 1914–18 sequence.

▷: Write a short story based either on Asquith's clerk or on Billy. Bring in the thoughts, motives and experiences of the young men, and give more details of their backgrounds.

Buttons   *Carl Sandburg*   12

Another American view of the European War. In the window of a Chicago newspaper office, Sandburg looks at a large war map, on which coloured buttons show the relative positions of armies. A cheerful young man climbs up to move the buttons, following some battle activity at the Front. The poet has a sudden mental picture of the actual cost in human suffering of that simple move.

Which phrases are the most telling in the savage contrast that Sandburg makes between the over-simplified civilian view of war and its reality?

Compare with Siegfried Sassoon's *Suicide in the Trenches* (p. 15).

The Night Patrol   *Arthur Graeme West*   12

Arthur Graeme West was killed at the Front in France in April, 1917. He left a few poems and the moving *Diary of a Dead Officer*, in which he records a disillusion with the war that brought him near to rebellion against the Army.

In February, 1916, he wrote in a letter:

I had an exciting time myself on a patrol in the 'no man's land' between the lines. A dangerous business, and most repulsive on account of the smells and appearance of the heaps of dead men that lie unburied there as they fell, on some attack or other, about four months ago. I found myself more interested than afraid . . .

What things in *No Man's Land* (the strip of ground between the Allied and German trenches on the Western Front) appeal to West's curiosity? What does he find horrific? Find some examples of 'black humour' in his description. What does this poem tell us about the pity and futility of war?

The Hero   *Siegfried Sassoon*   14

Siegfried Sassoon showed great courage in the trenches, winning the Military Cross. Stunned by the horrors of battle, Sassoon was invalided home from the trenches, and began to write sharp, biting poems as part of his personal crusade against war. He aimed to shock a complacent civilian public who falsely glorified the fighting.

In this poem, Sassoon takes the popular ideal of heroism, the 'supreme sacrifice', as his subject. What is the reaction of Jack's mother to the news that her son has been killed? Compare this with the attitude of *the Brother Officer*. How had Jack really behaved? What is Sassoon saying about the gap between soldiers and civilians?

▷ : Two letters home, written from the trenches in France:
one from Jack to his mother, boasting about his exploits, the other from a fellow officer to a friend telling the true story of Jack's cowardice.

Suicide in the Trenches   *Siegfried Sassoon*   15

The concise, powerful story of a young soldier who killed himself while serving at the Front.

What sort of person was he? What exactly did he do to himself and why? Why did no-one speak of him again? Why is Sassoon angry with the *smug-faced crowds* of civilians at home? What is his message to them?

Notice the force of the rhymes here, and the brilliance of the last line, - with its balanced abstract nouns, - that sums up the nightmare of the Western Front.

The Effect   *Siegfried Sassoon*   15
Press reports on the war were at their worst during 1915–17. To returning soldiers, their lies and distortions summed up the civilian 'war madness' that they so detested.

Sassoon borrows some newspaper sentences that seem to delight in the murderous effect of artillery bombardment. The soldier-narrator finds these phrases sick and pitiful when he thinks of the actuality of suffering in battle.

Study the last verse with its ghastly image of the fish (what exactly is meant here?), and its nursery-rhyme-like chorus (pick out the ugly contrasts). How would you describe the soldier's state of mind?

Great Men   *Siegfried Sassoon*   16
By July 1917, Sassoon's revulsion against the war reached such a pitch that he sent a protest statement to the press. Influential friends and his fine war record saved him from a military trial and a possible prison sentence. Instead, he was declared shell-shocked and sent to a hospital in Edinburgh where he met Wilfred Owen. Later he was reposted to the Front and was again wounded.

This poem is a bitter protest against those in authority, who create and direct wars, as contrasted with ordinary soldiers who fight and are killed.

It is a direct poem built around contrasts. Which contrasting ideas and phrases do you find most effective? It also uses precise adjectives and stinging rhymes. Which are most impressive?

The Target   *Ivor Gurney*   17
Ivor Gurney, poet and musician, served as a private at the Front. After the war, he suffered a mental breakdown and went to an asylum. But he continued to write, often recalling with haunting power his battle experiences.

Like Wilfred Owen's celebrated *Strange Meeting*, *The Target* describes the feelings of a soldier who has killed an enemy in a trench fight. Trace his shifting feelings. How does he sum them up in the last verse?

Not to keep   *Robert Frost*   18
A verse short story that describes, in plain, expressive language, a married couple's anxieties in wartime. The husband has been away fighting, and has been wounded. The simple, yet powerful, first sentence sets out the situtation. Who are *They* in this sentence?

What are the wife's feelings when she sees her husband again? Explain the lines *Everything seemed won, And all the rest for them permissible ease.*

The second verse changes the mood. What does *Enough, yet not enough,* mean? Notice the isolation of *Enough* for emphasis, and the cruel balancing phrase, *not enough*. Why has the man been sent home? On what condition has he returned to his wife? How do they both feel about this? Explain the last sentences, beginning *She dared no more . . .* What is the sinister meaning of the last line? How do you feel about *They* now?

▷ : The full story of this couple and their involvement in the war, beginning before the husband's departure for war service and going on after the poem's conclusion.

Spring Offensive   *Wilfred Owen*   19

Wilfred Owen died in action, at the age of 25, in the last week of the war. He had taken part in the Spring Offensive of 1917, an experience vividly outlined in a letter of May 14:

The sensations of going over the top are about as exhilarating as those dreams of falling over precipices ... When I looked back and saw the ground all crawling and wormy with wounded bodies, I felt no horror at all but only an immense exhaltation at having got through the barrage.

In the poem, soldiers wait to attack German positions on the other side of a *last hill*. While some sleep, others stand watching the ridge, feeling that death, *the end of the world*, is near. They gaze with envy at the simple life in insects and flowers around them. The sleepy heat is evoked by the onomatopoeia of words containing *z* and *ss* sounds: pick these out.

Verse three contains a strange idea: that buttercups and brambles have feelings and are anxious to hold men back from battle.

In verse four, the *little word* is the order to attack. The men say goodbye to the sun, seen by them as a kind of god, the centre and creator of life; *his whose bounty these have spurned* refers to the conventional Christian God, apparently rejected by disillusioned soldiers.

The last two verses describe the attack and its consequences. *sudden cups* are literally shell craters. They also suggest a Druid sacrifice: in other poems, Owen saw the war in these terms, with the younger generation being sacrificed by the older.

The Send-Off   *Wilfred Owen*   20

Owen may have been inspired by a *Times* correspondent of April 1918 who watched 'a dark mass of men' march across Westminster Bridge. The reporter regretted the glum spectacle of men going to war:

They neither sang nor whistled ... They marched in silence. ... Why should we not give the lads a real send-off, instead of smuggling them out of the country to which perhaps some of them will never return?

Although the soldiers in the poem have been given flowers, their departure seems like a plot against them. Which words and phrases suggest this? What point is made about the flowers? Why are the porter and the tramp included? What is the suggested fate of the soldiers? What is the point of the last five lines? Why are the roads *half-known*?

Owen worked hard to perfect the poem's opening. Here are some of his earlier versions:

Softly down darkening lanes they sang their way
And no word said.

Low voiced through darkening lanes, they sang their way
To the cattle-shed.

Down the deep, darkening lanes they sang their way
To the waiting train.

Why is the final version (that printed in this anthology) the best? Note especially the words *close darkening* and *siding-shed*.

Futility   *Wilfred Owen*   21

One of the few poems Owen saw published in his lifetime.

One bleak morning in the front line, an officer sees one of his men shot beside him. In shock, he gives an odd command: *Move him into the sun.* Just as the sun has woken him each morning in his home country, so it might now wake the dead soldier. What arguments does the officer use to explain his thinking? What work did the dead man do in civilian life? Which lines tell you this? What does the word *half-sown* tell us about his work?

Why mention *snow*? What is meant by *limbs, so dear achieved*? The *clays of a cold star* means the original chemical 'soup' from which the elements of life were created in the remote past of the Earth (called, poetically, a *star*).

Was it for this the clay grew tall?: according to the Biblical creation myth, mankind was moulded from clay. Owen comments on the long evolution of man, regretting that a human being, its end product, can be so quickly killed.

Trace the rhyme scheme. Owen uses 'half-rhymes', an echo effect he devised to give a firm shape, while avoiding the bounciness of ordinary rhyme.

The Armistice   *May Wedderburn Cannan*   22

May Cannan worked in France during the war, and wrote several remarkable poems about her experiences and a sad wartime romance. Here she describes a British government office in Paris and the effect that the news of the Armistice on November 11, 1918, has on the various girls working there.

What are the reactions of the girls? Why does the poet make all the girls anonymous? The poem has considerable atmosphere: which descriptive details build this?

▷: Descriptive writing: the day peace came. Imagine the effects on, say, a family at home, and on soldiers in the Line.

The Son   *Clifford Dyment*   23

A poem about the effect of war on the children of those who died in battle. Dyment lost his father as a small child. Years later, he is deeply moved to read a wartime letter from his father to his mother. He broods on the fate of his father, whom he sees almost as a stranger, and of other dead soldiers. History, even if this is a personal, *unfamous* kind, suddenly comes alive to him.

What was the condition of the letter? What was it about? *My luck is at the bottom of the sea* means the father had no luck at all.

In the second verse, the poet's reaction to the letter is to feel suddenly more alive: which words and phrases tell you this?

MCMXIV   *Philip Larkin*   23
Larkin is looking back on the war from half a century later. He has been studying old photographs of volunteers queuing outside recruiting offices on August Bank Holiday, 1914.

From the poignantly cheerful faces of the volunteers, Larkin's imagination moves out to picture England – towns, countryside, great houses, dusty white roads – before the war changed it for ever. He sees 1914 as a turning point in English history, the end of an age of peace and innocence.

List the aspects of the old England that Larkin lovingly evokes. Why are the shops shut? What are *Established names*? Which names of kings and queens were fashionable for children in 1914? Why were the pubs *open all day*? What are Domesday lines? Why was there dust behind limousines?

What is the effect of the Latin numerals in the title? (Such numerals are sometimes seen carved on First World War memorials.)

War Blinded   *Douglas Dunn*   25
The poet is thinking about the long suffering of a veteran of the war. Blinded in the trenches, the ex-soldier has spent over sixty years in an institution.

What contrasting pictures does the poet imagine of the time when the soldier volunteered in 1914, and of the day that he was wounded? What work has the soldier done during his sixty years in hospital? What impresses the poet about the old man? How do his thoughts about the blind ex-soldier help him with his own problems in life (*this lesser dark*)? What does he not understand about the old soldier? Does the poet think the old man is more or less fortunate than those who died in the war?

▷ : Thoughts of the blind soldier about his pre-war and war-time experiences, and about the changed world that he now lives in.

THE SECOND WORLD WAR

Epitaph on a Tyrant   *W. H. Auden*   26
Here Auden is probably thinking of the dictators – Hitler, Mussolini, Stalin – of the 1930s, but his poem is also a comment on tyrannical rulers of all ages.

The poem is a nice balance of grudging, qualified admiration, set against horror at the man and his type. What qualities of mind has the dictator? What especially is the secret of his rise to power? What is his great enthusiasm? Why do his ministers laugh at his jokes? What are the effects of his anger (*when he cried*)? What examples of tyrants from recent history can you think of?

Refugee Blues   *W. H. Auden*   26

Blues are a form of American jazz music expressing regret and sorrow. Auden uses the style of such music in this comment on European refugees, driven from their own countries by dictatorial governments. He is thinking particularly of Jews forced out of Germany by Hitler in the 1930s.

Each verse in the poem suggests a different aspect of the refugees' fate. What are the saddest aspects? What makes them most bitter? What do they envy in the world of nature? What causes them most fear?

▷: A story that describes the experiences of particular refugees.

Embassy   *W. H. Auden*   28

The first two verses set the elegant, peaceful scene of the negotiations: well-dressed, highly paid diplomats work in beautiful surroundings. How do the *cultured flowers* reflect the diplomats themselves? What does *drifted* suggest about the way they talk together? What point is made in the phrase *priced their shoes*?

The third and fourth verses describe the results of the discussions (*the issue of their charm*). What are *well-made implements for causing pain*? What is a *verbal error* here? Which words of violence contrast with the peace of the opening verses?

Night Raid   *Desmond Hawkins*   28

An impression of what the poet saw and heard in a London air-raid shelter and on the streets as people waited for a German bombing attack during the Blitz of 1940–41. The nervous atmosphere is finely recreated by a mixture of loud brashness and quiet unease in the Londoners' reactions.

Pick out these reactions in the various characters. Why does the dancing girl talk so much and so loudly? What are the effects of *Someone muttered* and *Someone whispered beside me*? Who are 'they' in *They're coming up from the east*? What are *the small hours*? What sort of ideas might be included in *plausible conjectures*? What does the metaphor in the last two lines tell you about the state of London?

▷: A conversation in which the people in the poem show their thoughts and feelings during the raid.

Days drawing in   *E. J. Scovell*   29

A tiny sketch of a woman's feelings during a German air-raid. She remembers the dread of night, and the German bombers that it brought. She recalls the intense relief of dawn, after she and her child had survived the danger.

What does *The days fail* mean? Which words catch the tensions before the raid? Which describe how the child is precious to the mother? Which express the relief of the morning?

▷ : Fill out the concise details of the poem into a more complete account of the mother's experience of the raid.

The Bombing of the Café de Paris, 1941   *Vernon Scannell*   29

The Café de Paris was a fashionable Piccadilly restaurant in London. The dance floor was underground and therefore considered safe during air-raids. On the evening of March 8, 1941, servicemen on leave and their sweethearts were dancing to the music of the well-known jazz-band leader, 'Snakehips' Johnson. As the popular tune, 'Oh Johnny', was being played, a bomb pierced the floors above and exploded at chest height among the dancers. Thirty-four people died and sixty were seriously injured.

Scannell dramatizes the incident by making a forceful juxtaposition of scenes before and after the bomb. Pick out some ideas, words and phrases which make this contrast. He also traces the fates of individuals. What happens to the people mentioned? What is the *shattered dove* (verse three)? To what is the explosion compared (verse four)? Why are the ambulances *blinkered* (last verse)? What is so ugly and surprising about the next-to-last verse?

▷ : Tell the story of the bombing, using detail from the poem, as if you were one of the participants in the incident.

The Evacuee   *R. S. Thomas*   31

The evacuation of children from British cities began on September 1, 1939.

The poem compares the disturbing war experiences of a small girl from the city with her recovery in the peace she finds as an evacuee on a Welsh farm.

Outline the feeling and observations of the girl from the time she wakes to her sitting down to breakfast. What is the *quilt* she wakes under? What is she waiting for as she lies in bed? What does she actually hear?

What metaphor is used in the second verse? What changes in the girl are described in the last verse? Which images from country life are used to illustrate these changes? What was the girl's *long dread*? What is the force of the last two lines?

▷ : Write a full story about an evacuee.

Vergissmeinnicht   *Keith Douglas*   32

Keith Douglas might be called the Wilfred Owen of the Second World War. He died, aged 24, during the D-Day landings in Normandy in June 1944, after fighting previously in North Africa.

Here Douglas thinks about a dead German soldier he found in the Libyan desert. He also describes him in his prose account of the war, *From Alamein to Zem Zem*:

I looked into the face of a man lying hunched up in a pit . . . He was like a cleverly posed waxwork ... The dust which powdered his face like an actor's lay on his wide open eyes. This picture filled me with useless pity.

What is most pathetic about the dead German? Which images are used to show the horror of the corpse? Why mention the photograph of his girl-friend and its written message? What is the point of the last verse? And the title?

The Battle   *Louis Simpson*   33

A poem about American infantrymen during the advance across Europe after D-Day in 1944. The setting is the Ardennes, in France, scene of the last major German counter-attack in 1944–45.

Which image describes the appearance of the front line at night? What are the worst aspects of this winter warfare? The last verse focuses on individual soldiers. What is most pathetic about them? How does the poet use the idea of the glowing cigarette in relation to the soldiers?

A Front   *Randall Jarrell*   34

Jarrell served in the American 8th Air Force, based in eastern England during the war. Its 'Flying Fortresses' made massive bombing attacks on Germany. The poem describes aircraft returning from such a raid.

Front here has two meanings: it is the new sort of battle line created by air war, and it is the changeable English weather that makes flying difficult.

Jarrell wrote his own note to this poem:

A front is closing in over a bomber base; the bombers, guided in by signals from the five towers of the radio range, are landing. Only one lands before the base is closed; the next fly south to fields that are still open. One plane's radio has gone bad – it still transmits, but doesn't receive – and this plane tries to land and crashes.

Which phrases and images make the bombers' landing vivid to us? What is so sad about the aircraft with the damaged radio? What are the *lives the season quenches* and what two meanings has *quenches* here? Why does the air *quiver* and why does the *east sky glow*?

▷: Write about this incident from the viewpoint of either, the men in the control tower, or, the bombing crew in the aircraft.

The Interrogation   *Edwin Muir*   34

As a British Council official, Muir travelled widely in Europe in 1945. Several of his poems describe the sense of unease and dislocation in war-torn countries like Germany and Czechoslovakia.

This poem might be set anywhere in German-occupied Europe during the war, or indeed, in any country with an oppressive regime. The experience of secret arrest, interrogation and disappearance is all too familiar to us.

The arrested people in the poem are in the grip of a nameless but threatening authority. They can see the familiar, everyday world still close at hand, although they are now cut off from it.

The drama of the poem springs from its contrasts: the precise detail of the scene and the soldiers, and the vagueness of the charge. What sort of people are the soldiers? How do the accused feel about the nearby landscape? Why mention the *careless lovers*? Why does the poet say the lovers are *wandering another star*?

Anne Frank Huis   *Andrew Motion*   35

The Frank family were German Jews, who had fled to Holland in 1933 to escape the persecution of Hitler's Nazis. When Holland was occupied by the Nazis in 1940, the Franks were again in danger, this time from the 'final solution': Hitler's plan for the mass extermination of European Jews in concentration camps. In July 1942, the family went into hiding in an attic over an Amsterdam warehouse. There they stayed for over two years, never leaving the rooms. Anne, thirteen in 1942, kept her.famous diary until August 1944, when the Franks were betrayed to the Germans. All the Franks, except Anne's father, died in the camps. Anne died of typhus in Belsen in March 1945. Her diary was published after the war, and the attic became a museum.

Motion writes about a visit to this museum and the feelings it arouses in him. He finds himself identifying with Anne, and appreciating her claustrophobia and fear. He realizes the importance of the sound of the nearby church clock in her silent life, and the strong hopes centred on the chalk line on a map that marked the Allied advance towards Holland in 1944.

What else does he find moving about his glimpse of the Frank attic? When he leaves, he realizes his difference from the Franks: what did they long to do that he finds so easy? How does what he sees outside the house reflect sadly on what Anne missed?

▷: After some research on Anne (the Diary is published by Pan, and a play version by Blackie), *either* write, from her point of view, about some of her feelings and experiences in the attic. *Or* imagine that you were in hiding from an enemy, as the Franks were. Describe you hide-out and a day in your life.

War Cemetery, Ranville   *Vernon Scannell*   36

The poet is visiting one of the many British war cemeteries in Normandy, France, near the 1944 D-Day beaches. He admires its immaculate order. What striking simile is used to describe the gravestones? He also compares the stones to soldiers: in what ways are they alike? What is sad about some of the stones? What does he find disagreeable, even sinister, about the well-tended flowers on the graves? Why does he mention children in the last verse? Their noise is compared, rather oddly, to shell bursts: what point is the poet making here about the dead soldiers?

AFTER WORLD WAR II

At the Bomb Testing Site   *William Stafford*   37

The first atomic bomb was tested by the Americans at Los Alamos, New Mexico, USA, on July 16, 1945. In August it was used to destroy the Japanese cities of Hiroshima and Nagasaki to end the Second World War.

In the poem, a lizard is waiting for an atomic explosion in the New Mexico desert. Imagine the picture that is created in verse one; how would you describe its atmosphere? In the second verse, the lizard is able to see *something farther off*. It is able to somehow foresee the consequences of the explosion: *an important scene acted in stone . . . at the flute end of consequences*. What is its prediction?

The lizard is a simpler, tougher life form. Why is the creature *ready for a change* and why does it *wait* and *grip hard* on the desert? Why does the poet mention *a continent without much on it* and *a sky that never cared less*?

Your Attention Please   *Peter Porter*   37

A fantasy about the beginning of some Third World War of the future. The poet imagines a final radio broadcast to the population at large by a government official.

Bitter criticism of the attitudes of authority towards a war using nuclear weapons is suggested by what is said and by what is left unsaid. List the points you find strange or cruel in the government instructions. Which points are intended to encourage the civilians? How is religion used in the speech? What effect does the mention of the *cuckoo in your perspex panel* have on the tone of the speech? What opinions does the government official have of his listeners?

What is missing from the speech? What opinion does the poet have of the speaker and his attitudes?

▷ : The conversation of two people who have heard this broadcast, including their reactions to it. *Or* extracts from the diary of a person who lives through this war crisis.

Home-Coming   *Bruce Dawe*   39

Australia contributed troops to and suffered casualties in the Vietnam War of 1965–73, supporting South Vietnam as it tried unsuccessfully to repel invasion from the Communist North.

This sad picture of dead soldiers being brought home by aircraft from the front could also apply to any recent modern war, to the Falklands conflict or to Lebanon.

What is strange and horrible in the details of the collection of the dead bodies in Vietnam? What is so bitter about the phrase, *those they can find*? Why mention the hair-styles of the dead men? How is the sound of the planes' engines used in the poem? How is this echoed in the picture of the dogs in Australian towns?

What comparisons are used to describe:

the surburban streets of cities;
the sending of telegrams to relatives of the dead men;
the sadness of relatives when they hear of the return of the dead soldiers?
What force is there in the phrase, *too late, too early*?

What were they like   *Denise Levertov*   40
Denise Levertov was one of the many protest poets writing in the 1960s when
the Americans were fighting in Vietnam. This poem takes the unusual form of
a series of questions and answers in which she looks into the nature of the
culture of the Vietnamese people.

What qualities does she find in their culture? What does she see as the
effects of war? How does she feel about the people and their suffering? Which
phrases do you find most powerful?

GENERAL QUESTIONS

1. Some of these poems look back on war. Write about three of these that you
   find interesting.
2. What various features of war make these poets feel angry or sad?
3. Choose three poems from this selection which seem to you to be the best
   and most powerful comments on war. Write about the poems, describing
   their content and method, and say why each impresses you.
4. What do these tell us about the experience and suffering of soldiers in war?
   Discuss four or five poems in detail.

THE
NATURAL WORLD

MAN AND NATURE

from Song of Myself

I think I could turn and live with animals, they are so
    placid* and self-contain'd,   mild
I stand and look at them long and long.

They do not sweat and whine about their condition,
They do not lie awake in the dark and weep for their sins,
They do not make me sick discussing their duty to God,
Not one is dissatisfied, not one is demented* with the mania   mad
    of owning things,
Not one kneels to another, nor to his kind that lived
    thousands of years ago,
Not one is respectable or unhappy over the whole earth.

Walt Whitman

Travelling through the Dark

Travelling through the dark I found a deer
dead on the edge of the Wilson River* road.   in Washington, U.S.A.
It is usually best to roll them into the canyon*:   deep valley or gorge
that road is narrow; to swerve might make more dead.

By glow of the tail-light I stumbled back of the car
and stood by the heap, a doe, a recent killing;
she had stiffened already, almost cold.
I dragged her off; she was large in the belly.

My fingers touching her side brought me the reason –
her side was warm; her fawn lay there waiting,
alive, still, never to be born.
Beside that mountain road I hesitated.

The car aimed ahead its lowered parking lights;
under the hood purred the steady engine.
I stood in the glare of the warm exhaust turning red;
around our group I could hear the wilderness listen.

I thought hard for us all – my only swerving –
then pushed her over the edge into the river.

William Stafford

The Jaguar

The apes yawn and adore their fleas in the sun.
The parrots shriek as if they were on fire, or strut
Like cheap tarts to attract the stroller with the nut.
Fatigued* with indolence*, tiger and lion

Lie still as the sun. The boa-constrictor's* coil
Is a fossil. Cage after cage seems empty, or
Stinks of sleepers from the breathing straw.
It might be painted on a nursery wall.

But who runs like the rest past these arrives
At a cage where the crowd stands, stares, mesmerized,*
As a child at a dream, at a jaguar hurrying enraged
Through prison darkness after the drills of his eyes

On a short fierce fuse. Not in boredom –
The eye satisfied to be blind in fire,
By the bang of blood in the brain deaf the ear –
he spins from the bars, but there's no cage to him

More than to the visionary* his cell:
His stride is wildernesses of freedom:
The world rolls under the long thrust of his heel.
Over the cage floor the horizons come.

Ted Hughes

tired, weary
laziness

large snake

hypnotized

religious hermit

To a Mare

Eager and gentle one,
the grass is springing
green where you used to walk.
The drought is over
and all the birds are singing.
The roads of spring are waiting,
eager and gentle one.

Such simple words as these –
words soft and easy –
I use, but you are dead.
You won't hear what I'm saying,
nor lift your head,
its dark long-tilted eyes,
from where you're lying
eager and gentle one.

Mare of the clean straight pace,
hide grey as mist or ghost,
what shall I tell your rider,
she who will miss you most?
Only, "All born must die;
all loved be lost?"

Say, Death I do not know.
Life, I knew well,
its forward urging thrust
that set me dancing,
the noise of its great show –
grass-tastes, the bit-bar's steel.
Tell her who rode me last
death's only nothing;
death has no taste at all.

Judith Wright

At Grass

The eye can hardly pick them out
From the cold shade they shelter in,
Till wind distresses tail and mane;
Then one crops grass, and moves about
– The other seeming to look on –
And stands anonymous* again.   without a name

Yet fifteen years ago, perhaps
Two dozen distances sufficed*   were enough
To fable them: faint afternoons
Of Cups and Stakes and Handicaps,
Whereby their names were artificed*   crafted
To inlay faded, classic Junes* –   horse racing seasons

Silks* at the start: against the sky   jockey's colours
Numbers and parasols: outside,
Squadrons of empty cars, and heat,
And littered grass: then the long cry
Hanging unhushed till it subside
To stop-press columns on the street.

Do memories plague their ears like flies?
They shake their heads. Dusk brims the shadows.
Summer by summer all stole away,
The starting-gates, the crowds and cries –
All but the unmolesting meadows.
Almanacked*, their names live; they   on racing calendars

Have slipped their names, and stand at ease,
Or gallop for what must be joy,
And not a fieldglass sees them home,
Or curious stop-watch prophesies*:   makes predictions
Only the groom, and the groom's boy,
With bridles in the evening come.

Philip Larkin

Sheep

The sheep has stopped crying.
All morning in her wire-mesh compound
On the lawn, she has been crying
For her vanished lamb. Yesterday they came.
Then her lamb could stand, in a fashion,
And make some tiptoe cringing* steps.   cowering
Now he has disappeared.
He was only half the proper size,
And his cry was wrong. It was not
A dry little hard bleat, a baby-cry
Over a flat tongue, it was human,
It was a despairing human smooth Oh!
Like no lamb I ever heard. Its hindlegs
Cowered in under its lumped spine,
Its feeble hips leaned towards
Its shoulders for support. Its stubby
White wool pyramid head, on a tottery neck,
Had sad and defeated eyes, pinched, pathetic,
Too small, and it cried all the time
Oh! Oh! staggering towards
Its alert, baffled, stamping, storming mother
Who feared our intentions. He was too weak
To find her teats, or to nuzzle up in under,
He hadn't the gumption*. He was fully   personal drive
Occupied just standing, then shuffling
Towards where she'd removed to. She knew
He wasn't right, she couldn't
Make him out. Then his rough-curl legs,
So stoutly built, and hooved
With real quality tips,
Just got in the way, like a loose bundle
Of firewood he was cursed to manage,
Too heavy for him, lending sometimes
Some support, but no strength, no real help.
When we sat his mother on her tail, he mouthed her teat,
Slobbered a little, but after a minute
Lost aim and interest, his muzzle wandered,

He was managing a difficulty
Much more urgent and important. By evening
He could not stand. It was not
That he could not thrive, he was born
With everything but the will –
That can be deformed, just like a limb.
Death was more interesting to him.
Life could not get his attention.
So he died, with the yellow birth-mucus*   slimy substance
Still in his cardigan.
He did not survive a warm summer night.
Now his mother has started crying again.
The wind is oceanic in the elms
And the blossom is all set.

Ted Hughes

The Stag

While the rain fell on the November woodland shoulder of
    Exmoor
While the traffic jam along the road honked and shouted
Because the farmers were parking wherever they could
And scrambling to the bank-top to stare through the tree-
    fringe
Which was leafless,
The stag ran through his private forest.

While the rain drummed on the roofs of the parked cars
And the kids inside cried and daubed their chocolate and
    fought
And mothers and aunts and grandmothers
Were a tangle of undoing sandwiches and screwed-round
    gossiping heads
Steaming up the windows,
The stag loped through his favourite valley.

While the blue horsemen down in the boggy meadow
Sodden nearly black, on sodden horses,
Spaced as at a military parade,
Moved a few paces to the right and a few to the left and felt
    rather foolish
Looking at the brown impassable river,
The stag came over the last hill of Exmoor.

While everybody high-kneed it to the bank-top all along
    the road
Where steady men in oilskins were stationed at binoculars,
And the horsemen by the river galloped anxiously this way
    and that
And the cry of hounds came tumbling invisibly with their
    echoes down through the draggle of trees,
Swinging across the wall of dark woodland,
The stag dropped into a strange country.

And turned at the river
Hearing the hound-pack smash the undergrowth, hearing
    the bell-note
Of the voice that carried all the others,
Then while his limbs all cried different directions to his
    lungs, which only wanted to rest,
The blue horseman on the bank opposite
Pulled aside the camouflage of their terrible planet.*   frightening alien world

And the stag doubled back weeping and looking for home
    up a valley and down a valley
While the strange trees struck at him and the brambles
    lashed him,
And the strange earth came galloping after him carrying
    the loll-tongued hounds to fling all over him
And his heart became just a club beating his ribs and his
    own hooves shouted with hounds' voices,
And the crowd on the road got back into their cars
Wet-through and disappointed.

Ted Hughes

The Meadow Mouse

1

In a shoe box stuffed in an old nylon stocking
Sleeps the baby mouse I found in the meadow,
Where he trembled and shook beneath a stick
Till I caught him up by the tail and brought him in,
Cradled in my hand,
A little quaker, the whole body of him trembling,
His absurd whiskers sticking out like a cartoon-mouse,
His feet like small leaves,
Little lizard-feet,
Whitish and spread wide when he tried to struggle away,
Wriggling like a miniscule* puppy.   very small

Now he's eaten his three kinds of cheese and drunk from his
    bottle-cap watering-trough –
So much he just lies in one corner,
His tail curled under him, his belly big
As his head; his bat-like ears
Twitching, tilting towards the least sound.

Do I imagine he no longer trembles
When I come close to him?
He seems no longer to tremble.

2

But this morning the shoe-box house on the back porch is
    empty.
Where has he gone, my meadow mouse,
My thumb of a child that nuzzled in my palm? –
To run under the hawk's wing,
Under the eye of the great owl watching from the elm-tree,
To live by courtesy of the shrike*, the snake, the tom-cat.   butcher-bird

I think of the nestling fallen into the deep grass,
The turtle gasping in the dusty rubble of the highway,
The paralytic stunned in the tub, and the water rising, –
All things innocent, hapless*, forsaken.   unlucky

Theodore Roethke

Conditions of Pain

At dusk my father brought a sparrow in.
One of its eyes was a blob of blood
caught on a thorn or slashed
by some cat. We put it in the greenhouse
with crumbs and a saucer of milk.
All we could do. But it was dead before dawn.

In Cardiff Market on the fish stall
there was this poor lobster
with its jaws tied by elastic
crawling over rocks in a glass case.
People looked at the lobster with curiosity
or fascination, as it blundered about.

I knew a tomcat in Westfield
so old it could hardly walk,
wheezing towards me for a stroke.
Day and night on a front doorstep
in cold and rain, dying in his yellow
sick eyes, wanting something to end.

In New Quay behind the Black Lion
a forgotten donkey stared back at me
from its barbed-wire patch without grass.
And on the screen inside the pub
a young seal was being clubbed to death
as it looked up at horror on the ice.

Images of pain, fragments of suffering
stored in my memory until I die.
Oh God, I say to myself, instinctively
for there is no one else to appeal to
as these things continue, everywhere, all the time.
Compassion* goes beyond compassion, and into pain.   pity

John Tripp

Death of a Whale

When the mouse died, there was a sort of pity;
The tiny, delicate creature made for grief.
Yesterday, instead, the dead whale on the reef
Drew an excited multitude to the jetty.
How must a whale die to wring a tear?
Lugubrious* death of a whale; the big   mournful
Feast for the gulls and sharks; the tug
Of the tide simulating life still there,
Until the air, polluted, swings this way
Like a door ajar from a slaughterhouse.
Pooh! pooh! spare us, give us the death of a mouse
By its tiny hole; not this in our lovely bay
– Sorry, we are, too, when a child dies;
But at the immolation* of a race, who cries?   sacrificial killing

John Blight

A Butterfly

Even under the shed there's something outdoors
about the work. One side stands open

to stars and wind. You pause on your barrow to watch
dawn come up, or a shower across the city.

You're never bricked in. On slack shifts in summer
men wander off along overgrown sidings, embankments,

for a sun and a glance through the *Mirror*: a couple
have planted a vegetable-garden back of Humberstone Coal
    Wharf.

Grass invades. Dustiest corners are settled
with unauthorised flowers. The Grain Shed sparrows

strut plundering leaking sacks, great rats
buck-jump away from right under your feet.

On a fine day wagons trundle in hung with glittering
waterdrops: somewhere rain is falling.

Even one bleak night, surrounded
by foggy blackness, and cartons, crates,

rolls of netting stacked up on the shed-platform,
hard graft, something broke in when old Gumble found

in the straw that wadded a cased-up carboy* of acid   large glass bottle
a sleepy butterfly. It crawled

on to his palm. 'Beautiful little beggar,
in't it?' It fluttered in his sour beer breath.

'Look at this, Jacko. Red Admiral.' Wherever
he carried it, cupped precious in his hands,

men stopped, gathering under wan lights:
blue overalls, stubbled faces focused on

a butterfly, straw strewn upon the concrete,
and birds starting racketing for the new day in the girders.

Andrew Waterman

To paint a Water Lily

A green level of lily leaves
Roofs the pond's chamber and paves

The flies' furious arena: study
These, the two minds of this lady.

First observe the air's dragonfly
That eats meat, that bullets by

Or stands in space to take aim;
Others as dangerous comb the hum

Under the trees. There are battle-shouts
And death-cries everywhere hereabouts

But inaudible*, so the eyes praise   cannot be heard
To see the colours of these flies

Rainbow their arcs, spark, or settle
Cooling like beads of molten metal

Through the spectrum. Think what worse
Is the pond-bed's matter of course;

Prehistoric bedragonned times
Crawl that darkness with Latin names,

Have evolved no improvements there,
Jaws for heads, the set stare,

Ignorant of age as of hour –
Now paint the long-necked lily-flower

Which, deep in both worlds, can be still
As a painting, trembling hardly at all

Though the dragonfly alight,
Whatever horror nudge her root.

Ted Hughes

Throwing a Tree

New Forest

The two executioners stalk along over the knolls*,   small hills
Bearing two axes with heavy heads shining and wide,
And a long limp two-handled saw toothed for cutting
great boles*,   tree trunks
And so they approach the proud tree that bears the death-
mark on its side.

Jackets doffed they swing axes and chop away just
above ground,
And the chips fly about and lie white on the moss and
fallen leaves;

Till a broad deep gash in the bark is hewn* all the way   cut
    round,
And one of them tries to hook upward a rope, which at last
    he achieves.

The saw then begins, till the top of the tall giant shivers:
    The shivers are seen to grow greater each cut than
    before:
    They edge out the saw, tug the rope; but the tree only
    quivers,
And kneeling and sawing again, they step back to try
    pulling once more.

Then, lastly, the living mast sways, further sways: with
    shout
    Job and Ike rush aside. Reached the end of its long
    staying powers
    The tree crashes downward: it shakes all its neighbours
    throughout,
And two hundred years' steady growth has been ended in
    less than two hours.

Thomas Hardy

Trees at the Arctic Circle

(Salix Cordifolia – Ground willow)

They are 18 inches long
or even less
crawling under rocks
grovelling among the lichens*   mossy plants
bending and curling to escape
making themselves small
finding new ways to hide
Coward trees
I am angry to see them
like this

not proud of what they are
bowing to weather instead
careful of themselves
worried about the sky
afraid of exposing their limbs
like a Victorian married couple

I call to mind great Douglas firs
I see tall maples waving green
and oaks like gods in autumn gold
the whole horizon jungle dark
and I crouched under that continual night
But these
even the dwarf shrubs of Ontario
mock them
Coward trees

And yet – and yet –
their seed pods glow
like delicate grey earrings
their leaves are veined and intricate
like tiny parkas*   Eskimo jackets
They have about three months
to ensure the species does not die
And that's how they spend their time
unbothered by any human opinion
just digging in here and now
sending their roots down down down
And you know it occurs to me
    about 2 feet under
these roots must touch permafrost*   ice layer that never
ice that remains ice forever   melts
and they use it for their nourishment
use death to remain alive

I see that I've been carried away
in my scorn of the dwarf trees
most foolish in my judgements
To take away the dignity
    of any living thing
even tho it cannot understand
    the scornful words

is to make life itself trivial
and yourself the Pontifex Maximus*   chief priest
    of nullity*   nothingness
I have been stupid in a poem
I will not alter the poem
but let the stupidity remain permanent
as the trees are
in a poem
the dwarf trees of Baffin Island.*   in Canadian Arctic

Alfred Purdy

Municipal Gum

Gumtree in the city street,
Hard bitumen* around your feet,   asphalt
Rather you should be
In the cool world of leafy forest halls
And wild bird calls.
Here you seem to me
Like that poor cart-horse
Castrated, broken, a thing wronged,
Strapped and buckled, its hell prolonged,
Whose hung head and listless mien* express   bearing
Its hopelessness.
Municipal gum, it is dolorous*   sad
To see you thus
Set in your black grass of bitumen –
O fellow citizen,
What have they done to us?

Kath Walker

THE SEASONS

Spring Nature Notes

The sun lies mild and still on the yard stones.

The clue is a solitary daffodil – the first.

And the whole air struggling in soft excitements
Like a woman hurrying into her silks.
Birds everywhere zipping and unzipping
Changing their minds, in soft excitements,
Warming their wings and trying their voices.

The trees still spindle bare.

Beyond them, from the warmed blue hills
An exhilaration* swirls upward, like a huge fish.   happy excitement

As under a waterfall, in the bustling pool.

Over the whole land
Spring thunders down in brilliant silence.

Ted Hughes

The Trees

The trees are coming into leaf
Like something almost being said:
The recent buds relax and spread.
Their greenness is a kind of grief.

Is it that they are born again
And we grow old? No, they die too.
Their yearly trick of looking new
Is written down in rings of grain.

Yet still the unresting castles thresh
In fullgrown thickness every May.
Last year is dead, they seem to say.
Begin afresh, afresh, afresh.

Philip Larkin

Adlestrop

Yes. I remember Adlestrop –
The name, because one afternoon
Of heat the express-train drew up there
Unwontedly*. It was late June.   not in the usual way

The steam hissed. Someone cleared his throat.
No one left and no one came
On the bare platform. What I saw
Was Adlestrop – only the name.

And willows, willow-herb, and grass,
And meadowsweet, and haycocks dry,
No whit* less still and lonely fair   not a bit
Than the high cloudlets in the sky.

And for that minute a blackbird sang
Close by, and round him, mistier,
Farther and farther, all the birds
Of Oxfordshire and Gloucestershire.

Edward Thomas

Cut Grass

Cut grass lies frail;
Brief is the breath
Mown stalks exhale,
Long, long the death

It dies in the white hours
Of young-leafed June
With chestnut flowers,
With hedges snowlike strewn,

White lilac bowed,
Lost lanes of Queen Anne's lace,
And that high-builded cloud
Moving at summer's pace.

Philip Larkin

The Cyclist

Freewheeling down the escarpment past the unpassing
    horse*   White Horse in
                                                        Wiltshire
Blazoned* in chalk the wind he causes in passing   painted as on a shield
Cools the sweat of his neck, making him one with the sky,

In the heat of the handlebars he grasps the summer
Being a boy and to-day a parenthesis*   something set aside
Between the horizon s brackets; the main sentence
Is to be picked up later but these five minutes
Are all to-day and summer. The dragonfly
Rises without take-off, horizontal,
Underlining itself in a sliver of peacock light.

And glaring, glaring white
The horse on the down moves within his brackets,
The grass boils with grasshoppers, a pebble
Scutters from under the wheel and all this country
Is spattered white with boys riding their heat-wave,
Feet on a narrow plank and hair thrown back,

And a surf of dust beneath them. Summer, summer –
They chase it with butterfly nets or strike it into the deep
In a little red ball or gulp it lathered with cream
Or drink it through closed eyelids; until the bell
Left-right-left gives his forgotten sentence
And reaching the valley the boy must pedal again
Left-right-left but meanwhile
For ten seconds more can move as the horse in the chalk
Moves unbeginningly calmly
Calmly regardless of tenses and final clauses
Calmly unendingly moves.

Louis Macneice

Reluctance

Out through the fields and the woods
    And over the walls I have wended*;   made my way
I have climbed the hills of view
    And looked at the world, and descended;
I have come by the highway home,
    And lo, it is ended.

The leaves are all dead on the ground,
    Save those that the oak is keeping
To ravel* them one by one   disentagle
    And let them go scraping and creeping
Out over the crusted snow,
    When others are sleeping.

And the dead leaves lie huddled and still,
    No longer blown hither and thither;
The last lone aster* is gone;   Michaelmas daisy
    The flowers of the witch-hazel wither;
The heart is still aching to seek,
    But the feet question 'Whither?'

Ah, when to the heart of man
    Was it ever less than a treason
To go with the drift of things,
    To yield with a grace to reason,
And bow and accept the end
    Of a love or a season?

Robert Frost

Trio

Coming up Buchanan Street,* quickly, on a sharp winter   in Glasgow
    evening
a young man and two girls, under the Christmas lights–
The young man carries a new guitar in his arms,
the girl on the inside carries a very young baby,
and the girl on the outside carries a chihuahua*.   miniature dog
And the three of them are laughing, their breath rises
in a cloud of happiness, and as they pass
the boy says, 'Wait till he sees this but!'
The chihuahua has a tiny Royal Stewart tartan coat like a
    teapot-holder,
the baby in its white shawl is all bright eyes and mouth like
    favours in a fresh sweet cake,
the guitar swells out under its milky plastic cover, tied at
    the neck with silver tinsel tape and a brisk sprig of
    mistletoe.
Orphean* sprig! Melting baby! Warm chihuahua!   an offshoot from the
The vale of tears is powerless before you.   legendary Greek
                                            musician, Orpheus

Whether Christ is born, or is not born, you
put paid to fate, it abdicates*   resigns
                  under the Christmas lights.
Monsters of the year
go blank, are scattered back,
can't bear this march of three.

– And the three have passed, vanished in the crowd
(yet not vanished, for in their arms they wind
the life of men and beasts, and music,
laughter ringing them round like a guard)
at the end of this winter's day.

Edwin Morgan

NOTES AND
SUGGESTIONS FOR WORK

▷ : Topic for imaginative writing arising from ideas in the poem.

MAN AND NATURE

from: Song of Myself   *Walt Whitman*   56
This is a fragment of the American writer's long poem, *Song of Myself*. In this extract, Whitman compares the life of animals with that of people. What does he think about animals? What various faults does he see in human beings? Which faults does he hate and despise the most?

▷ : Your own contrast between the lives of people and animals.

Travelling through the Dark   *William Stafford*   56
The poet shows pity and sorrow for a deer killed on a mountain road in Washington State, USA.
    Seeing the deer in his path, he stops his car on a night journey to push the dead creature into the river below. He pauses, finding she is pregnant. How does he know this? He hesitates (a *swerving* from the obvious course of action). Should he try to rescue the living fawn from the dead mother's stomach, or should he leave it die? What is his final decision, as chooser of life or death for the unborn fawn? Was he right or wrong?

▷ : An encounter with a wild creature.

The Jaguar   *Ted Hughes*   57
Hughes wrote this poem while working as a dish-washer at London Zoo. He could see the jaguar's cage from his sink in the café.
    He compares the jaguar with other creatures in the zoo. Which words or phrases suggest the relative crudeness or dullness of these other animals? In what way is the boa-constrictor's coil like a fossil?
    How do people react to the jaguar? What impresses the poet about the jaguar's response to its immediate circumstances? What does *prison darkness* mean? Why is the jaguar compared to *the visionary in his cell*? What metaphor is used in the phrase: *on a short fierce fuse*? What do the last two lines mean? How would you describe the poet's feelings about the jaguar?

To a Mare   *Judith Wright*   58
The Australian poet, Judith Wright, thinks about a well-loved horse that has recently died. What physical details of the mare are given to us?

Spring, the beginning of the long season of open-air activity, has returned and yet the mare is now dead. Who, besides the poet, will miss the creature now? What consolation does the poet offer this person? What general conclusions about life and death does the poem give us?

▷: Your own piece about the life and death of a well-loved animal.

At Grass   *Philip Larkin*   59

The poet watches two retired race-horses standing at dusk under the trees in the corner of a meadow where they now live quiet days.

He contrasts their present obscure retirement with the fame and attention they once had as famous winners of classic races fifteen years before. Pick out words and phrases that express this.

Anonymous (nameless) is the key word to describe their present state. They have shed the names that made them celebrated: even the word 'horse' is avoided in the poem. What metaphor is contained in the sentence: *they have slipped their names*. Now one *can hardly pick them out*. In what various ways did people look at them in the past? Why do they gallop now? Why are the meadows *unmolesting*? *The wind distresses tail and mane*: which two words are cleverly run together in *distresses*?

The poet recreates scenes from great race meetings of the past in *faded, classic Junes*. Which details make this atmosphere? What is *the long cry*? How exactly does it *subside* to the street?

Look at the phrases *cold shade, dusk brims the shadows* and *in the evening come*. What do they, and the quiet rhythm of the last verse, suggest about the future of the horses?

Sheep   *Ted Hughes*   60

Hughes based this poem on his experiences of the harsh realities of farming. Here he ponders the mystery of life and death in the exactly detailed story of a sick lamb and its mother.

What is pathetic about the mother? What defects did Hughes see in the lamb? What is most disconcerting about the creature? Hughes tried to make the lamb feed but *He was managing a difficulty much more urgent and important*. What does this mean? Why did he die?

Why does the poet mention the wind in the trees and the blossom, at the end of the poem?

Pick out examples of the poet's vigorous use of words and the images used to describe the lamb.

▷: A sad story involving an animal, domestic or wild.

The Stag   *Ted Hughes*   61

This description of a Devon stag hunt contrasts the behaviour of human beings and animals. How are the humans presented to us? What impression do we form of their behaviour? How do we see the stag? Pick out words and phrases which help create these impressions.

In the fifth verse, the stag and the horseman confront each other. What is the animal's reaction to the human world? Why is it a *terrible planet*?

In the last verse, the sequence of *and*s conveys the fear and urgency of the stag as it tries to escape. What final comment do the last two lines make?

▷: Tell this story from the alternative viewpoints of the huntsmen and the hunted stag. Invent a conclusion.

The Meadow Mouse   *Theodore Roethke*   63

The poet describes an attempt to help and care for a lost wild creature. Tell the story of the finding of the mouse and the provisions Roethke made for it. What comparisons are used to create a vivid picture of the mouse?

What does the poet fear when he finds the creature missing next day? What general feeling about creatures (and people) is aroused in him by this experience of caring for the mouse?

▷: Describe experiences of your own in trying to help and rear lost or injured wild creatures.

Conditions of Pain   *John Tripp*   64

The poet lists some upsetting incidents, involving living creatures, that he has witnessed. Describe these in your own words and try to say exactly what upsets the poet so much. How long will he remember these incidents?

What point does he make in his appeal to God? What is the point of the last line? What is the tone of the last verse?

▷: What makes you most angry about man's treatment of other living creatures?

Death of a Whale   *John Blight*   65

Blight contrasts the death of a whale stranded on a reef with that of a mouse. People pitied the mouse. But what prevents the local people from pitying the whale, although they are at first excited by the spectacle?

In the last two lines, the poet draws a conclusion from his pictures: what is this (*Immolation of a race* probably refers specifically to the mass slaughter of Jews by Hitler in World War II.)

A Butterfly   *Andrew Waterman*   65

Before he went to university, Andrew Waterman had several casual jobs, including one on the railway in Leicestershire. This is one of several railway poems.

What images of natural beauty does he focus on? How does he contrast the workaday environment of the yard and natural things? What does the poem suggest to you about the men who work there and about their feelings towards what they see and experience?

▷: Your own observations of the natural world while you are in school or at work outside school.

To paint a Water Lily   *Ted Hughes*   66
Hughes contemplates a pool covered with lily leaves, something usually seen as a calm, peaceful subject, but he knows the peace is an illusion. The air above the pond, *the flies' arena*, is full of insects waging a pitiless battle for survival against each other. Which are the most fearsome of these creatures? If you could magnify the insects' sounds, you would hear *battle shouts and death cries*. What images does the poet use to define the vivid appearance of the flies?

Below the lilies is a second space, the underwater chamber. What are the creatures with Latin names that lurk there? What is so horrific about them?

Joining the two worlds is the lily, with its long-necked flower in the air and its roots below the surface. It remains still and beautiful even when the worst of the air and water creatures come near it.

What general comment does the poem make about the natural world?

Throwing a tree   *Thomas Hardy*   67
Hardy expresses what many of us feel about the cutting down of a great, old tree.

The dignity and grandeur of the tree is contrasted with the swift, crude work of the men who fell it. What effect on our thinking does the word *executioners* have? Find other words and phrases which make the tree seem like a person.

Which line sums up the pitiful message of the poem?

Trees at the Arctic Circle   *Alfred Purdy*   68
This Canadian poet describes the dwarf willow-trees that just manage to survive in the Canadian tundra, the near-barren wastes towards the Arctic where even the subsoil is frozen.

How does he feel towards these small trees? What words express his attitude? What are the qualities of trees which he admires? Where does the poem show a shift in his viewpoint? What does he find to admire in the dwarf trees in the second part of the poem? The tree roots dig down to the permafrost. Why does the poet say they *use death to remain alive*?

He finally appreciates that even the most unprepossessing trees, like other living things, have their own mysterious power and dignity. How does he think of himself in view of his misjudgement?

Municipal Gum   *Kath Walker*   70
Kath Walker is the first Aboriginal poet to become well-known to white Australians.

The gum is the characteristic Australian tree. Where does the poet see this particular gum tree? Which phrases contrast its present position with the environment that the poet thinks it should have? Why is the tree like the old horse seen nearby on the city street? In the last two lines, the poet compares the tree to her own position as an Aborigine in modern Australia: in what ways are they alike? Who are *they* in the last line?

THE SEASONS

Spring Nature Notes   *Ted Hughes*   71

A picture of the beginning of spring in the countryside. There is little to see – a single daffodil or the still bare trees – but the new season is sensed as excitement. This is conveyed by Hughes in strange, bold comparisons; what is compared to what in these? The last line contains a clash of opposite ideas. Can you identify them?

The Trees   *Philip Larkin*   71

Larkin tries to demolish the idea that each spring is a kind of rebirth for us – that, just as there is fresh growth in tree and plant, so there is a renewal in ourselves. Instead, the fresh foliage is only a *trick of looking new*. The tree is really getting older, just as we are: cut a branch and you will see the rings of growth that mark the years of the tree's age.

Despite this, the splendid trees, covered with new green (to what are they compared?) still suggest to us that they, and we, are making a fresh start on life each spring. What sound does the repeated *afresh* suggest in the last line?

▷ : (on this and the previous poem) Your own images of the first signs of spring in town or country. Be up-to-date and honest in your observations.

Adlestrop   *Edward Thomas*   72

Thomas remembers stopping at this tiny village on a train one hot day, and he carefully reconstructs in his memory the atmosphere of high summer.

Thomas wrote the poem in January 1915: thus he is looking back to the last summer of peace. A 1914 notebook recorded the actual incident:

> A glorious day ... we stopped at Adlestrop, through the willows could be heard a chain of blackbirds' songs at 12.45 and one thrush and no man seen, only a hiss of engine letting off steam ... banks of long grass, willowherb and meadowsweet, extraordinary silence between two periods of travel – looking out on grey dry stones between metals and the shining metals and over it all the elms willows and long grass – one man clears his throat – a greater than rustic silence ... Stop only for a minute till signal is up.

Compare the details of the poem with this note: what has Thomas added or taken away?

The *Yes* on the first line suggests the poem is half a conversation. Someone has asked him about the curiously named village. His memory gradually recalls that moment of summer. Notice how the short sentences and long pauses (both at full stops, and between verses one and two), actually build the effect of silence into the poem.

Two senses are dominant in the description. What does Thomas hear at the station? What does he see? (His vision, like a film shot, opens out from the station sign to include a wider and wider landscape: the several *and*'s in the last verses reflect this opening out.) In the last verse, he becomes aware of birdsong on a widening scale, until he thinks he can hear birds of several counties: the visual word *mist* is used to define this sound effect.

Cut Grass   *Philip Larkin*   73

Larkin reflects on the hay harvest (the *cut grass*), and the brevity of the delicious scent of the new-mown fields. Around this he builds a picture of the beauties of early summer. *White* is a key word to join his ideas: trace its use from *white hours* (of bright sunlight) to the *high-builded cloud*.

What do you think is Larkin's theme in this poem? Compare with Molly Holden's *Photograph of Haymaker, 1890*, (p. 150).

▷ : (on this and the previous poem) Your own summer picture built from details observed through the five senses.

The Cyclist   *Louis Macneice*   73

As a schoolboy Macneice enjoyed spare-time cycle rides over the Downs near his school at Marlborough in Wiltshire:

We skimmed down southwards over the chalk country . . . upon wheels, we were free, . . .

In the poem he reconstructs five minutes from his boyhood summer. As he rushes downhill, he passes the famous 'White Horse', carved into the chalky hillside. Its frozen gallop suggests to him the idea that time stops as he races along on his bicycle. The moment becomes a parenthesis, something set apart from ordinary life, as a statement in brackets is set aside in a sentence.

What does he see and feel as he *grasps the summer* in these five minutes of speeding down the hill? What does he imagine other boys doing at this moment of high summer?

At the end of the poem, he reaches the bottom of the hill and resumes ordinary life, the life outside the 'brackets' of this intense experience.

Reluctance   *Robert Frost*   74

Frost describes the melancholy of autumn. Although he longs to continue, his walks and explorations of summer must come to an end. The last leaves have fallen; the last flowers died. Pick out the words that suggest decay and death.

Frost is unwilling to face the dying of the year in the same way that people are reluctant to accept the end of a love affair. Both ideas hint, perhaps, at the final extinction of man in death. In this way, the poet sees autumn as a metaphor for human mortality.

Contrast with Keats' *Ode to Autumn*, which sees this season as a time of richness and fulfilment.

▷ : The pleasant or sad features of autumn in town or country.

Trio   *Edwin Morgan*   75

Morgan uses a brief, chance encounter with three young people, seen in the Christmas crowds on a Glasgow street, to comment on winter, and also on our attitude to life and death. The poem is a firm answer to those who see life only as a *vale of tears*.

Whom, do you suppose, are the young people going to see? What are they carrying? Why does the poet see these things as particularly significant? What do you think the *monsters of the year* are? How does Christmas fit into this experience? How are the ideas of winter and death linked here?

GENERAL QUESTIONS

1. According to the observations of these poets, what lessons does the natural world of creatures and plants teach mankind?
2. Show how the poets express pity for the life of the natural world and resentment at man's treatment of it.
3. What do the poets find pleasurable, sad, or interesting about the English seasons?
4. Which of the poems in this selection show the competitive or violent side of natural life?
5. Which of these observations or descriptions of the natural world seem to you unusual or particularly effective? Try to explain why you found them of interest.

LOVE AND MARRIAGE

LOVE

On the Ridgeway

Thinking of those who walked here long ago
On this greenway in summer and in snow
She said, 'This is the oldest road we tread,
The oldest in the world?' 'Yes, love,' I said.

Andrew Young

After a Romantic Day

   The railway bore him through
An earthen cutting out from a city:
   There was no scope for view,
Though the frail light shed by a slim young moon
   Fell like a friendly tune.

   Fell like a liquid ditty,
And the blank lack of any charm
   Of landscape did no harm.
The bald steep cutting, rigid, rough,
   And moon-lit, was enough
For poetry of place: its weathered face
Formed a convenient sheet whereon
The visions of his mind were drawn.

Thomas Hardy

That night when joy began

That night when joy began
Our narrowest veins to flush,
We waited for the flash
Of morning's levelled gun.

But morning let us pass,
And day by day relief
Outgrows his nervous laugh,
Grown credulous* of peace,   too ready to believe in

As mile by mile is seen
No trespasser's reproach,
And love's best glasses reach
No fields but are his own.

W. H. Auden

Girl's Song

I was so happy that I hardly knew it
Nor ever guessed that life was not all play,
And little dreamt I'd live to see the dawning
Of such a day –
Oh, why, why should it be
That suddenly
Life should seem strange and terrible to me?

I'd never cared for lads like other lasses
Nor heeded overmuch what they might say,
And little dreamt I'd live to see the dawning
Of such a day –
Oh, why, why should it be
That suddenly
A lad's word should mean life and death to me?

Wilfrid Gibson

First Frost

A girl is freezing in a telephone booth,
huddled in her flimsy coat,
her face stained by tears
and smeared with lipstick.

She breathes on her thin little fingers.
Fingers like ice. Glass beads in her ears.

She has to beat her way back alone
down the icy street.

First frost. A beginning of losses,
the first frost of telephone phrases.

It is the start of winter glittering on her cheek,
the first frost of having been hurt.

Andrei Voznesensky
    (translated Stanley Kunitz)

Always Marry an April Girl

Praise the spells and bless the charms,
I found April in my arms.
April golden, April cloudy,
Gracious, cruel, tender, rowdy;
April soft in flowered languor*,   soft, quiet mood
April cold with sudden anger,
Ever changing, ever true –
I love April, I love you.

Ogden Nash

Meeting at Night

The grey sea and the long black land;
And the yellow half-moon large and low;
And the startled little waves that leap
In fiery ringlets from their sleep,
As I gain the cove with pushing prow*,   pointed front of a boat
And quench its speed in the slushy sand,

Then a mile of warm sea-scented beach;
Three fields to cross till a farm appears:
A tap at the pane, the quick sharp scratch
And blue spurt of a lighted match,
And a voice less loud, through its joys and fears,
Than the two hearts beating each to each!

Robert Browning

Under the Waterfall

'Whenever I plunge my arm, like this,
In a basin of water, I never miss
The sweet sharp sense of a fugitive* day   fleeting
Fetched back from its thickening shroud of gray.
   Hence the only prime
   And real love-rhyme
   That I know by heart,
   And that leaves no smart,
Is the purl* of a little valley fall*   sound
About three spans wide and two spans tall   water-fall
Over a table of solid rock,
And into a scoop of the self-same block;
The purl of a runlet that never ceases
In stir of kingdoms, in wars, in peaces;
With a hollow boiling voice it speaks
And has spoken since hills were turfless peaks.'

'And why gives this the only prime
Idea to you of a real love-rhyme?
And why does plunging your arm in a bowl
Full of spring water, bring throbs to your soul?'

'Well, under the fall, in a crease of the stone,
Though where precisely none ever has known,
Jammed darkly, nothing to show how prized,
And by now with its smoothness opalized*,   the glass turned milky-
   Is a drinking-glass: white by the water
   For, down that pass
   My lover and I
   Walked under a sky
Of blue with a leaf-wove awning of green,
In the burn of August, to paint the scene,
And we placed our basket of fruit and wine,
By the runlet's rim, where we sat to dine;
And when we had drunk from the glass together,
Arched by the oak-copse from the weather,
I held the vessel to rinse in the fall,
Where it slipped, and sank, and was past recall,
Though we stooped and plumbed the little abyss*   water-filled hole
With long bared arms. There the glass still is.
And, as said, if I thrust my arm below
Cold water in a basin or bowl, a throe*   pang
From the past awakens a sense of that time,
And the glass we used, and the cascade's rhyme.
The basin seems the pool, and its edge
The hard smooth face of the brook-side ledge,
And the leafy pattern of china-ware
The hanging plants that were bathing there.

'By night, by day, when it shines or lours*,   is dark and threatening
There lies intact that chalice* of ours,   glass
And its presence adds to the rhyme of love
Persistently sung by the fall above.
No lip has touched it since his and mine
In turns there from sipped lovers' wine.'

Thomas Hardy

Green

The dawn was apple-green,
   The sky was green wine held up in the sun,
The moon was a golden petal between.

She opened her eyes, and green
   They shone, clear like flowers undone
For the first time, now for the first time seen.

D. H. Lawrence

Beyond the Last Lamp

While rain, with eve in partnership,
Descended darkly, drip, drip, drip,
Beyond the last lone lamp I passed
   Walking slowly, whispering sadly,
   Two linked loiterers, wan*, downcast: pale
Some heavy thought constrained each face,
And blinded them to time and place.

The pair seemed lovers, yet absorbed
In mental scenes no longer orbed
By love's young rays. Each countenance*   facial expression
   As it slowly, as it sadly
   Caught the lamplight's yellow glance,
Held in suspense a misery
At things which had been or might be.

When I retrod that watery way
Some hours beyond the droop of day,
Still I found pacing there the twain*   two people
   Just as slowly, just as sadly,
   Heedless of the night and rain.
One could but wonder who they were
And what wild woe detained them there.

Though thirty years of blur and blot
Have slid since I beheld that spot,
And saw in curious converse there
   Moving slowly, moving sadly
   That mysterious tragic pair,
Its olden look may linger on –
All but the couple; they have gone.

Whither? Who knows, indeed. . . . And yet
To me, when nights are weird and wet,
Without those comrades there at tryst*   lovers' meeting
   Creeping slowly, creeping sadly,
   That lone lane does not exist.
There they seem brooding on their pain,
And will, while such a lane remain.

Thomas Hardy

Where shall we go?

Waiting for her in the usual bar
He finds she's late again.
Impatience frets at him,
But not the fearful, half-sweet pain he knew
So long ago.

That cherished perturbation* is replaced   mental agitation
By styptic* irritation   that stops bleeding
And, under that, a cold
Dark current of dejection moves
That this is so.

There was a time when all her failings were
Delights he marvelled at:
It seemed her clumsinesss,
Forgetfulness and wild non-sequiturs*   irrelevant remarks
Could never grow

Wearisome, nor would he ever tire
Of doting* on those small   adoring
Blemishes that proved
Her beauty as the blackbird's gloss affirms
The bridal snow.

The clock above the bar records her theft
Of time he cannot spare;
Then suddenly she's here.
He stands to welcome and accuse her with
A grey 'Hello'.

And sees, for one sly instant, in her eyes
His own aggrieved* dislike   annoyed
Wince back at him before
Her smile draws blinds. 'Sorry I'm late,' she says.
'Where shall we go?'

Vernon Scannell

A Winter's Tale

Yesterday the fields were only grey with scattered snow,
And now the longest grass-leaves hardly emerge;
Yet her deep footsteps mark the snow, and go
On towards the pines at the hill's white verge*.   edge

I cannot see her, since the mist's pale scarf
Obscures the dark wood and the dull orange sky;
But she's waiting, I know, impatient and cold, half
Sobs struggling into her frosty sigh.

Why does she come so promptly, when she must know
She's only the nearer to the inevitable* farewell?   unavoidable
The hill is steep, on the snow my steps are slow –
Why does she come, when she knows what I have to tell?

D. H. Lawrence

Dismissal

To this day I remember
that alcove: flaked coffee-coloured
paint, an ashtray spilling, two
vodkas. As she broke it
with one sentence, I remember looking
left at an old lady
pouring her stout. Funny,
how at turning-points and news of grief
we do the ordinary. 'Oh,'
I said, as if my little finger
had been cut. It was more
embarrassment than shock. Three years
it took for her words to sink in.

John Tripp

An Anniversary

Endlessly the stream slides past,
Jellies each white flat stone
Which stares through its slithering window at
The sky's smeared monotone*.   one colour

Two willow leaves glide smoothly on
The water's shimmering skin;
Inches apart they float along,
The distance never changing.

Once, on a branch in the sun, they danced
And often touched each other;
They will not touch each other again,
Not now, not ever.

Vernon Scannell

MARRIAGE

Wedding-Wind

The wind blew all my* wedding-day,   the wife is the narrator
And my wedding-night was the night of the high wind;
And a stable door was banging, again and again,
That he must go and shut it, leaving me
Stupid in candlelight, hearing rain,
Seeing my face in the twisted candlestick,
Yet seeing nothing. When he came back
He said the horses were restless, and I was sad
That any man or beast that night should lack
The happiness I had.

      Now in the day
All's ravelled* under the sun by the wind's blowing.   confused
He has gone to look at the floods, and I
Carry a chipped pail to the chicken-run,
Set it down, and stare. All is the wind
Hunting through clouds and forests, thrashing
My apron and the hanging cloths on the line.
Can it be borne, this bodying-forth* by wind   giving an outward
Of joy my actions turn on, like a thread   shape
Carrying beads? Shall I be let to sleep
Now this perpetual morning shares my bed?
Can even death dry up
These new delighted lakes, conclude
Our kneeling as cattle by all-generous waters?

Philip Larkin

Gardening Sunday

She brushes her hair out in the sun.
This could be a young girl – such absorption,

and the lifted forearm plumped. All day
we have moved together through roses, currants,
silently. Now she tucks up like a girl
on the kitchen step, gathering on her hair

the dwindling lustre of this Sunday,
while I wash hands, and make the tea for her.

The jars stand full of fruit. People spend
their fifty years going no farther.

Brian Jones

Love Songs in Age

She kept her songs, they took so little space.
    The covers pleased her:
One bleached from lying in a sunny place,
One marked in circles by a vase of water,
One mended, when a tidy fit had seized her,
    And coloured, by her daughter –
So they had waited, till in widowhood
She found them, looking for something else, and stood

Relearning how each frank submissive* chord
    Had ushered in
Word after sprawling hyphenated* word,
And the unfailing sense of being young
Spread out like a spring-woken tree, wherein
    That hidden freshness sung,
That certainty of time laid up in store
As when she played them first. But, even more,

music that made her give in to its power

words divided to fit the music

The glare of that much-mentioned brilliance, love,
　　Broke out, to show
Its bright incipience* sailing above,   first stages
Still promising to solve, and satisfy,
And set unchangeably in order. So
　　To pile them back, to cry,
Was hard, without lamely admitting how
It had not done so then, and could not now.

Philip Larkin

Devonshire Street W.1

The heavy mahogany door with its wrought-iron screen
　　Shuts. And the sound is rich, sympathetic, discreet.
The sun still shines on this eighteenth-century scene
　　With Edwardian faience* adornments – Devonshire   clay decorations
　　　Street.

No hope. And the X-ray photographs under his arm
　　Confirm the message. His wife stands timidly by.
The opposite brick-built house looks lofty and calm
　　Its chimneys steady against a mackerel sky.

No hope. And the iron knob of this palisade*   fence of iron railings
　　So cold to the touch, is luckier now than he
'Oh merciless, hurrying Londoners! Why was I made
　　For the long and the painful deathbed coming to me?'

She puts her fingers in his, as, loving and silly,
　　At long-past Kensington dances she used to do
'It's cheaper to take the tube to Piccadilly
　　And then we can catch a nineteen or a twenty-two.'

Sir John Betjeman

The Ghost

'Who knocks?' 'I, who was beautiful,
    Beyond all dreams to restore,
I, from the roots of the dark thorn am hither*.   here
    And knock on the door.'

'Who speaks?' 'I – once was my speech
    Sweet as the bird's on the air,
When echo lurks by the waters to heed;
    'Tis I speak thee fair.'

'Dark is the hour!' 'Ay, and cold.'
    'Lone is my house,' 'Ay, but mine?'
'Sight, touch, lips, eyes yearned* in vain.'   longed for
    'Long dead these to thine . . .'

Silence. Still faint on the porch
    Brake the flames of the stars.
In gloom groped a hope-wearied hand
    Over keys, bolts, and bars.

A face peered. All the grey night
    In chaos of vacancy shone;
Nought* but vast sorrow was there –   nothing
    The sweet cheat gone.

Walter de la Mare

The Voice

Woman much missed, how you call to me, call to me,
Saying that now you are not as you were
When you had changed from the one who was all to me,
But as at first, when our day was fair.

Can it be you that I hear? Let me view you, then,
Standing as when I drew near to the town
Where you would wait for me: yes, as I knew you then,
Even to the original air-blue gown!

Or is it only the breeze, in its listlessness
Travelling across the wet mead* to me here,   field
You being ever dissolved to wan* wistlessness*,   pale
Heard no more again far or near?   state of being forgotten

    Thus I; faltering forward,
    Leaves around me falling,
Wind oozing thin through the thorn from norward,
    And the woman calling.

Thomas Hardy

NOTES AND
SUGGESTIONS FOR WORK

▷ : Topic for imaginative writing arising from ideas in the poem.

LOVE

On the Ridgeway   *Andrew Young*   86

The Ridgeway is a prehistoric track, once used for carrying flint from Norfolk to the south coast of England.

The girl in this short poem is walking along the path with her lover. He interprets her question in two ways. What are they? Which word is the most important and powerful in his answer? What comment does the poem make about human love?

After a Romantic Day   *Thomas Hardy*   86

A young man leaves the city on a train after spending some time with a girlfriend. From the window, he stares out onto an ugly railway cutting. Which words create the impression of ugliness? He projects his happy thoughts of the last day onto this drab background, just as images in a film are thrown onto a screen. Which phrases describe the man's happiness?

Hardy was trying to show that a beautiful natural scene is not the only suitable background for love.

▷ : The happy scenes that the young man imagined.

That night when joy began   *W. H. Auden*   87

A love lyric expressed in strange but vivid imagery. The lovers' intense joy in each other washes, like a liquid, into their *narrowest veins*. Their bond is expressed in terms of territory that they own together. To their surprise, no one else invades or threatens it. The sun (traditionally the return of day has been seen as an enemy that divides lovers), is compared to the gleam of a hostile gun: which word connects *sun* to *gun*? But, as the days pass, and their journey of love continues, they come to believe that there are no dangers ahead, that the whole landscape belongs to them.

What does *credulous of peace* mean? Why does the poet mention a *nervous laugh* in verse two. What are *love's best glasses* in verse three?

Trace the rhyme scheme. What is strange about it? Compare with Wilfred Owen's *Futility* (p. 21): Auden was one of the few poets to imitate Owen's invention.

Girl's Song   *Wilfrid Gibson*   87

What has changed? Why is the girl surprised by this? What is the *lad's word* that means *life and death* to her?

First Frost   *Andrei Voznesensky*   88

A translation of a poem by a Russian writer.

Describe the girl, giving details of her appearance and behaviour. Why is she in the telephone box? What is happening to her? What do you think the 'phone conversation is about? What does *a beginning of losses* mean? What is the ambiguity in *the start of winter glittering on her cheek*? (Note that tears freeze in the intense outdoor cold of the Russian winter.)

Trace the metaphor of ice and frost through the poem. How is it related to the girl's feelings?

▷ : Write a complete story about the girl, filling in more background and giving details of her sad relationship. The story might end with the scene in the poem. Include the conversations on the telephone. You need not use Russian names or settings.

Always Marry an April Girl   *Ogden Nash*   88

A light-hearted, but tender, love poem. The girl is not necessarily called April: her various moods remind the poet of the month of April, that is, fresh and spring-like but very unpredictable in its weather.

What is meant in the first line? What are some of the varied moods of the girl? How exactly is she *soft in flowered languor*? How does the writer feel about her sudden temper?

Meeting at Night   *Robert Browning*   89

Where is the story taking place? What does the man see, hear and feel on his journey? Why are the waves like *fiery ringlets*? How are the secrecy and tensions of the meeting suggested?

▷ : *Either*, the full story behind this poem, *or*, your own story, 'A Secret Romance'.

Under the Waterfall   *Thomas Hardy*   89

Hardy's poem is based upon an actual incident from the early days of his courtship with Emma Gifford, who later became his wife. In her autobiography, *Some Recollections*, Emma writes:

Often we walked down the beautiful valley (of the Valency river in Cornwall) . . . by narrow pathways . . . with a sparkling little brook going the same way, into which we once lost a tiny picnic tumbler, and there it is to this day no doubt between two small boulders.

The story is told from the point of view of Emma. As she plunges her arms in a basin to wash, the shock of the water causes her to recall an intense memory. A picture of the streams flowing over rocks in the valley comes to her, and then the day when she and her lover sat by the waterfall and lost the glass. What word is used in the poem for the picnic tumbler? What words are used to describe its present state? What does this suggest about her love?

To what does Emma compare the flow of the stream in the first section of the poem? Who speaks the second section of the poem? What does Emma remember of the scene that surrounded the picnic? Would you say that the tone of the poem was happy, sad, romantic or regretful?

Green   *D. H. Lawrence*   91

This is one of the poems that Lawrence wrote about his wife, Frieda, at the time of their elopement together in 1912. He sees the woman as if for the first time, and the world about her seems newly made.

A series of images expresses these feelings. What comparisons are made in these images? What is the effect of the repetition in the last line? Why is the word *green* repeated so often?

Beyond the Last Lamp   *Thomas Hardy*   91

In Hardy's novel *Tess of the d'Urbevilles*, Tess and Angel are seen by a cottager:

Two lovers . . . walking very slowly, . . . one behind the other, as in a funeral procession . . . Returning late, he passed them again in the same field, progressing just as slowly, and as regardless of the hour and of the cheerless night as before.

This poem also describes a pair of lovers seen by Hardy when he was living in London in the 1870s. What picture do you form of them? What similarities are there between the unnamed lovers of the poem and Tess and Angel? Which lines are almost identical in each verse? How do these contribute to the mood of the poem? How does the poet think of this scene thirty years later?

▷: Who are the *mysterious tragic pair*. What is the story behind their strange meeting?

Where shall we go?   *Vernon Scannell*   92

A picture of the end of a romantic relationship. As the man waits for the girl, whom he is beginning to tire of, various emotions pass through his mind. What are these? (A styptic substance stops bleeding. Irritation is styptic because it stops the bleeding – or emotional disturbance – of love.)

When he was in love with the girl, he used to think her faults charming. What are these faults? These faults used to set off her beauty: what image is used to describe this effect? Notice the long pause before *wearisome*.

When the girl finally arrives late, he greets her. Which word qualifies this greeting so that he *accuses* her? What, to his surprise, does he see in her eyes? What image describes her pretended pleasure at seeing him?

What double meaning is there in her final question and also, in the title?

A Winter's Tale　*D. H. Lawrence*　93
In this poem, a girl is waiting at the edge of the woods for her lover. Why is the girl early and the man late for the appointment? Which words and phrases suggest the attitude of each of them to the situation? What does the landscape suggest to us about the relationship?

Compare with *First Frost* by Voznesensky, (p. 88).

Dismissal　*John Tripp*　94
A young man remembers the pain of being told by his girlfriend that she wishes to end their relationship.

The pain is intense, deep and long-lasting. What immediate effect does it have on his response to the girl? By contrast, as often happens when a person is shocked, his mind photographs his surroundings. For years after he remembers a scatter of disconnected things around him. What are these? When did the break finally register in his mind?

▷: (On this and the two previous poems): Story: 'The end of the affair.'

An Anniversary　*Vernon Scannell*　94
The poet is reflecting on a broken relationship. He listlessly stares at a river, seeing in it pictures of his own mood and recent experience.

Look at the first verse about the river. Which words that describe the water also suggest the poet's sad mood? Try to define what *jellies* and *slithering window* mean exactly.

He sees two fallen willow leaves floating along the river. To what does he compare them? What several points of comparison does he develop? What is the idea suggested in the last line?

MARRIAGE

Wedding-Wind　*Philip Larkin*　95
The narrator is the newly-wed wife of a farmer. The wind, that blew during her wedding-day, becoming a gale that night, seems to represent to the girl her new joy and the tremendous change that has come over her life. The whole world seems excited: doors bang; animals are restless; clothes flap wildly on the line.

Which phrases and images describe her emotions? What does she mean by *perpetual morning*? How does she feel, in the midst of her joy, about other people and living creatures? Even the floods caused by the storm seem a part of her contentment. How exactly? How does the girl feel about the future of her marriage?

▷: Your own imaginative picture of the girl's wedding and her feelings about it.

Gardening Sunday   *Brian Jones*   96
A man and his wife have spent a Sunday picking and bottling fruit. The eventless but delightful day is described in quiet, serene verse.

There are two themes: the closeness of the relationship (which phrases emphasize this?) and fruitfulness (which ideas underline this?). What picture of the wife is created? What does the final sentence mean?

Love Songs in Age   *Philip Larkin*   96
An elderly widow comes across some old song music-sheets that she used to play over with her husband, when they were both young. The sheets have been hidden away in a drawer, and she comes upon them again with pleasurable surprise. How, in the layout of verses one and two, does the poet express her quiet shock at finding them? What marks of the passing of time are on the sheets?

As she scans the notes and hyphenated words (they are printed to match the music), the past is suddenly recalled to her. In verse two, what feelings from the past does she experience again.

What does *spring-woken* mean? What did love promise to do in the girl's life? As the woman puts the sheets back, what does she have to admit that love has not done?

▷: Consider some objects (old books, toys, holiday souvenirs, pieces of clothing, records etc.) that revive memories of your past. Try to describe the memories and feelings connected with these objects.

Devonshire Street W.1   *Sir John Betjeman*   97
The husband of this elderly couple has been to see a doctor in the Devonshire Street Clinic in London. It is confirmed that he has a fatal disease and faces a painful death. We share his feelings and observations, as he and his wife, stunned by the news, emerge onto the street.

The emphasis on *shuts* suggests that the door is seen metaphorically. What other door is shutting on the man? The clinic door sounds *rich, sympathetic, discreet.* Who else sounded like this?

Which phrase is given emphasis in verse two? How do the details of the London street contrast with the man's fears? In verse three, what strange thoughts does he have about the fence and about the passers-by?

How does the wife react? As she takes his hand, what picture from the past comes to her mind?

▷: The wife's account of this experience.

The Ghost   *Walter de la Mare*   98
A lonely man imagines that his dead wife returns from her grave (beneath a thorn tree in the graveyard) to visit him. He thinks he hears her knocking at the door and speaking to him.

In the first three verses, who speaks which words? (Try reading the poem in parts.) What simile describes the wife? With what does it connect her? In the third verse, what three reasons does the man give for not opening the door to let her in? What are her replies?

In the last two verses, the man is finally convinced that she is actually there. Why? His *hope-wearied hand* undoes the locks and bolts. He looks out into the night. What does he see outside? Which words express his sadness and disappointment?

The Voice   *Thomas Hardy*   99
The poet thinks he hears the voice of his *much missed* woman, his dead wife, calling to him. What does she seem to be saying? He longs to see her as she used to be while she waited for him at Launceston Station, when he came to visit her in Cornwall in 1870. What vivid detail does he remember about her?

Then he begins to doubt the voice. What might it be? Which words express his melancholy in this verse? What happens to the vision of his wife?

The last verse breaks the smooth, waltz rhythm of the poem, with its unusual three syllable rhymes, *call to me/all to me*. It shows Hardy alone, an old man, stumbling forward on his journey. What do his surroundings suggest about his present feelings and about his future? What is the force of the last line?

Compare with Walter de la Mare's *The Ghost*, (p. 98).

GENERAL QUESTIONS

1. What do these poets tell us about the happiness or the unhappiness connected with human love?
2. Which do you find the most impressive poem about marriage? Consider both the style and content of the poem.
3. Some of these poems are about remembered relationships. Write about three of them, commenting on their content and technique, especially their imagery.

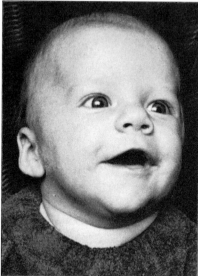

PEOPLE

CHILDREN AND PARENTS

Morning Song

Love set you going like a fat gold watch.
The midwife slapped your footsoles, and your bald cry
Took its place among the elements.

Our voices echo, magnifying your arrival. New statue
In a draughty museum, your nakedness
Shadows our safety. We stand round blankly as walls.

I'm no more your mother
Then the cloud that distils a mirror to reflect its own slow
Effacement* at the wind's hand.   wiping out

All night your moth breath
Flickers among the flat pink roses. I wake to listen:
A far sea moves in my ear.

One cry, and I stumble from bed, cow-heavy and floral
In my Victorian nightgown.
Your mouth opens clean as a cat's. The window square

Whitens and swallows its dull stars. And now you try
Your handful of notes;
The clear vowels rise like balloons.

Sylvia Plath

Children's Song

We live in our own world,
A world that is too small
For you to stoop and enter
Even on hands and knees,
The adult subterfuge*.
And though you probe and pry
With analytic* eye,
And eavesdrop* all our talk
With an amused look,
You cannot find the centre
Where we dance, where we play,
Where life is still asleep
Under the closed flower,
Under the smooth shell
Of eggs in the cupped nest
That mock the faded blue
Of your remoter heaven.

way out of a difficulty

trying to work out
meanings

overhear

R. S. Thomas

Janet Waking

Beautifully Janet slept
Till it was deeply morning. She woke then
And thought about her dainty-feathered hen,
To see how it had kept.

One kiss she gave her mother,
Only a small one gave she to her daddy
Who would have kissed each curl of his shining baby;
No kiss at all for her brother.

'Old Chucky, old Chucky!' she cried,
Running across the world upon the grass
To Chucky's house, and listening. But alas,
Her Chucky had died.

It was a transmogrifying* bee   changing in a magical
Came droning down on Chucky's old bald head   manner
And sat and put the poison. It scarcely bled,
But how exceedingly

And purply did the knot
Swell with the venom* and communicate   poison
Its rigor*! Now the poor comb stood up straight   rigidity caused by
But Chucky did not.   poison

So there was Janet
Kneeling on the wet grass, crying her brown hen
(Translated far beyond the daughters of men)
To rise and walk upon it.

And weeping fast as she had breath
Janet implored us, 'Wake her from her sleep!'
And would not be instructed in how deep
Was the forgetful kingdom of death.

John Crowe Ransom

For Cathy, on going to turn out her light

Climbing the stairs, mid-ocean blue,
I enter your room like entering an event:

dolls lopsided against walls, attired
in fancy-dress, blind-drunk with startling hair;
plasticine blob-men from a nordic* dream   from Norse legend
crawling over the waste-white of a desk;
mother's fifties' flouncy petticoats
and gold dance shoes, careless after the Ball;
a three-ply paper beach-hat, splodged with roses;
a chessman laid to sleep in a three-inch cradle,
his crowned head soft on tissue; four dolls
learning to read; a landscape pieced from felt
with a flock of sheep scissored from a napkin.

My dreams are secret, footpadding through darkness
for fear the day arrest them. You scatter
dreams through the world and let them take their chance.
You sleep now, with the bedside lamp still glaring,
knowing your dolls still read, your gold shoes dance.

Brian Jones

Discord in Childhood

Outside the house an ash-tree hung its terrible whips,
And at night when the wind rose, the lash of the tree
Shrieked and slashed the wind, as a ship's
Weird rigging in a storm shrieks hideously.

Within the house two voices arose, a slender lash
Whistling she-delirious* rage, and the dreadful sound   a woman's raving
Of a male thong booming and bruising, until it had drowned
The other voice in a silence of blood, 'neath the noise of the
    ash.

D. H. Lawrence

Fern Hill

Now as I was young and easy under the apple boughs
About the lilting house and happy as the grass was green,
    The night above the dingle* starry,   wooded valley
        Time let me hail and climb
    Golden in the heydays of his eyes,
And honoured among wagons I was prince of the apple
    towns
And once below a time I lordly had the trees and leaves
        Trail with daisies and barley
    Down the rivers of the windfall light.

And as I was green and carefree, famous among the barns
About the happy yard and singing as the farm was home,
   In the sun that is young once only,
      Time let me play and be
   Golden in the mercy of his means,
And green and golden I was huntsman and herdsman, the
   calves
Sang to my horn, the foxes on the hills barked clear and
   cold,
      And the sabbath* rang slowly   Sunday
   In the pebbles of the holy streams.

All the sun long it was running, it was lovely, the hay
Fields high as the house, the tunes from the chimneys, it
   was air
   And playing, lovely and watery
      And fire green as grass.
   And nightly under the simple stars
As I rode to sleep the owls were bearing the farm away,
All the moon long I heard, blessed among stables, the
   nightjars
   Flying with the ricks, and the horses
      Flashing into the dark.

And then to awake, and the farm, like a wanderer white
With the dew, come back, the cock on his shoulder; it was
   all
   Shining, it was Adam and maiden,
      The sky gathered again
   And the sun grew round that very day.
So it must have been after the birth of the simple light
In the first, spinning place, the spellbound horses walking
   warm
   Out of the whinnying green stable
      On to the fields of praise.

And honoured among foxes and pheasants by the gay house
Under the new made clouds and happy as the heart was
   long,
   In the sun born over and over,
      I ran my heedless ways,

My wishes raced through the house high hay
And nothing I cared, at my sky blue trades, that time
      allows
In all his tuneful turning so few and such morning songs
   Before the children green and golden
         Follow him out of grace,

Nothing I cared, in the lamb white days, that time would
      take me
Up to the swallow thronged loft by the shadow of my hand,
   In the moon that is always rising,
         Nor that riding to sleep
   I should hear him fly with the high fields
And wake to the farm forever fled from the childless land.
Oh as I was young and easy in the mercy of his means,
         Time held me green and dying
      Though I sang in my chains like the sea.

Dylan Thomas

Carrickfergus

I was born in Belfast between the mountain and the
      gantries*   crane towers
   To the hooting of lost sirens and the clang of trams:
Thence to Smoky Carrick in County Antrim
   Where the bottle-neck harbour collects the mud which
      jams

The little boats beneath the Norman castle,
   The pier shining with lumps of crystal salt;
The Scotch Quarter was a line of residential houses
   But the Irish Quarter was a slum for the blind and halt*.   crippled

The brook ran yellow from the factory stinking of chlorine,
   The yarn-mill called its funeral cry at noon;
Our lights looked over the lough* to the lights of Bangor   arm of the sea
   Under the peacock aura of a drowning moon.

The Norman* walled this town against the country
    To stop his ears to the yelping of his slave
And built a church in the form of a cross but denoting
    The list* of Christ on the cross in the angle of the nave.

I was the rector's son, born to the anglican order,
    Banned for ever from the candles* of the Irish poor;
The Chichesters* knelt in marble at the end of a transept
    With ruffs about their necks, their portion sure.

The war* came and a huge camp of soldiers
    Grew from the ground in sight of our house with long
Dummies hanging from gibbets* for bayonet practice
    And the sentry's challenge echoing all day long;

A Yorkshire terrier ran in and out by the gate-lodge
    Barred to civilians, yapping as if taking affront:
Marching at ease and singing 'Who Killed Cock Robin?'
    The troops went out by the lodge and off to the Front.

The steamer was camouflaged that took me to England –
    Sweat and khaki in the Carlisle train;
I thought that the war would last for ever and sugar
    Be always rationed and that never again

Would the weekly papers not have photos of sandbags
    And my governess not make bandages from moss
And people not have maps above the fireplace
    With flags on pins moving across and across –

Across the hawthorn hedge the noise of bugles,
    Flares across the night,
Somewhere on the lough was a prison ship for Germans,
    A cage across their sight.

I went to school in Dorset, the world of parents
    Contracted* into a puppet world of sons
Far from the mill girls, the smell of porter*, the salt-mines
    And the soldiers with their guns.

Louis Macneice

Marginal glosses:

Norman kings of England
leaning
Catholic faith
rich English land-owners
1914–18 war
gallows
shrank
beer

Rough

My parents kept me from children who were rough
Who threw words like stones and who wore torn clothes.
Their thighs showed through rags. They ran in the street
And climbed cliffs and stripped by the country streams.

I feared more than tigers their muscles like iron
Their jerking hands and their knees tight on my arms.
I feared the salt coarse pointing of those boys
Who copied my lisp behind me on the road.

They were lithe*, they sprang out behind hedges   supple
Like dogs to bark at my world. They threw mud
While I looked the other way, pretending to smile.
I longed to forgive them, but they never smiled.

Stephen Spender

My Mother

Reg wished me to go with him to the field.
I paused because I did not want to go;
But in her quiet way she made me yield,
Reluctantly, for she was breathing low.
Her hand she slowly lifted from her lap
And, smiling sadly in the old sweet way,
She pointed to the nail where hung my cap.
Her eyes said: I shall last another day.
But scarcely had we reached the distant place,
When over the hills we heard a faint bell ringing.
A boy came running up with frightened face –
We knew the fatal news that he was bringing.
I heard him listlessly*, without a moan,   without any reaction
Although the only one I loved was gone.

II

The dawn departs, the morning is begun,
The Trades* come whispering from off the seas,   winds
The fields of corn are golden in the sun,
The dark-blue tassels fluttering in the breeze;
The bell is sounding and the children pass,
Frog-leaping, skipping, shouting, laughing shrill,
Down the red road, over the pasture-grass,
Up to the schoolhouse crumbling on the hill.
The older folk are at their peaceful toil,
Some pulling up the weeds, some plucking corn,
And others breaking up the sun-baked soil.
Float, faintly-scented breeze, at early morn
Over the earth where mortals sow and reap –
Beneath its breast my mother lies asleep.

Last night I heard your voice, mother,
    The words you sang to me
When I, a little barefoot boy,
    Knelt down against your knee.

And tears gushed from my heart, mother,
    And passed beyond its wall,
But though the fountain reached my throat
    The drops refused to fall.

'Tis ten years since you died, mother,
    Just ten dark years of pain,
And oh, I only wish that I
    Could weep just once again.

Claude McKay

Digging

Between my finger and my thumb
The squat pen rests; snug as a gun.

Under my window, a clean rasping sound
When the spade sinks into gravelly ground:
My father, digging. I look down

Till his straining rump among the flowerbeds
Bends low, comes up twenty years away
Stooping in rhythm through potato drills
Where he was digging.

The coarse boot nestled on the lug, the shaft
Against the inside knee was levered firmly.
He rooted out tall tops, buried the bright edge deep
To scatter new potatoes that we picked
Loving their cool hardness in our hands.

By God, the old man could handle a spade.
Just like his old man.

My grandfather cut more turf in a day
Than any other man on Toner's bog.
Once I carried him milk in a bottle
Corked sloppily with paper. He straightened up
To drink it, then fell to right away

Nicking and slicing neatly, heaving sods
Over his shoulder, going down and down
For the good turf. Digging.

The cold smell of potato mould, the squelch and slap
Of soggy peat, the curt cuts of an edge
Through living roots awaken in my head.
But I've no spade to follow men like them.

Between my finger and my thumb
The squat pen rests.
I'll dig with it.

Seamus Heaney

Long Distance

Though my mother was already two years dead
Dad kept her slippers warming by the gas,
put hot water bottles her side of the bed
and still went to renew her transport pass.

You couldn't just drop in. You had to phone.
He'd put you off an hour to give him time
to clear away her things and look alone
as though his still raw love were such a crime.

He couldn't risk my blight* of disbelief   unpleasant influence
though sure that very soon he'd hear her key
scrape in the rusted lock and end his grief.
He *knew* she'd just popped out to get the tea.

I believe life ends with death, and that is all.
You haven't both gone shopping; just the same,
in my new black leather phone book there's your name
and the disconnected number I still call.

Tony Harrison

I was not there

The morning they set out from home
I was not there to comfort them
the dawn was innocent with snow
in mockery – it is not true
the dawn was neutral was immune
their shadows threaded it too soon
they were relieved that it had come
I was not there to comfort them

One told me that my father spent
a day in prison long ago
he did not tell me that he went
what difference does it make now
when he set out when he came home
I was not there to comfort him
and now I have no means to know
of what I was kept ignorant

Both my parents died in camps*   German concentration
I was not there to comfort them   camps
I was not there they were alone
my mind refuses to conceive
the life the death they must have known
I must atone* because I live   make amends
I could not have saved them from death
the ground is neutral underneath

Every child must leave its home
time gathers life impartially*   without favouring
I could have spared them nothing since   anyone
I was too young – it is not true
they might have lived to succour* me   help
and none shall say in my defence
had I been there to comfort them
it would have made no difference

Karen Gershon

from Autobiography

I

flags and bright funnels of ships
walking with my mother over the Seven Bridges
and being carried home too tired
frightened of the siren of the ferryboat
or running down the platform on the Underground
being taken over the river to see the big shops at Christmas
the road up the hill from the noisy dockyard
and the nasty smell from the tannery you didn't like going past
steep road that made your legs tired
up the hill from the Co-op the sweetshop the
                                 blue-and-white-tiled pub
Grandad's allotment on the lefthand side
behind the railings curved at the top
cobblestone path up the middle to the park
orderly rows of bean canes   a fire burning   sweetpeas tied
                                          up on strings

up to Our House
echoing flagyard entry between the two rows of houses
brick buttresses like lumps of cheese against the backyard walls
your feet clang and echo on the flags as you run the last few
                                          yards
pulling your woolly gloves off
shouting to show Grandad what you've just been bought
him at the door tall like the firtree in the park
darkblue suit gleaming black boots shiny silver watch chain
striped shirt no collar on but always a collarstud
heavy grey curled moustache that tickles when he picks you
                                         up to kiss you
sometimes shouting angry frightening you
till you see the laughter in his countryman's blue eyes

2

round redbrick doorway
yellow soapstone step cleaned twice a week
rich darkred linopattern in the polished lobby
front room with lace runners and a piano that you only go in
                                                on Sundays
or when someone comes to tea
Uncle Bill asleep in his chair coming in smelling of beer and
                                                horses
limping with the funny leg he got in the war
Grandma always in a flowered apron
the big green-and-red parrot frightening you with his sudden
                                                screeches
the two little round enamelled houses on either side of the
                                                fireplace
big turquoise flowered vase in the middle
the grate shining blackleaded cooking smell from the oven
                                                next to it

big black sooty kettle singing on the hob
fireirons in the hearth
foghorns and hooters
looking out of the kitchen window
seeing the boats on the bright river
and the cranes from the dockyards

3

coming back the taxidriver doesn't know where the street is
the allotments at the foot of the hill
gone now
great gaunt terraces of flats
scarred with graffiti
instead
the redbrick houses tiny falling apart
the whitewashed backyard
where you could smell lily of the valley through the privethedge
                                                round the tiny garden
on your way to the lavatory at the end
empty dirty overgrown now

backdoor banging in the wind
grandmother grandfather both dead in hospital
one windowpane broken dirty lace curtains flapping
the funny little flights of steps
the secret passages in the park
pink sandstone steps overhung with trees up the side of the hill
overgrown or demolished
the big seacaptain's house where I used to go for a present
                              every Christmas
forgotten
remembering
lying in bed
in the dark crying listening to my mother and father argue
wind banging a shutter
indoors somewhere
dead eyes looking out from flyblown photographs
empty mirrors reflecting the silence

Adrian Henri

from Ancestors

Every Friday morning my grandfather
left his farm of canefields*, chickens, cows,   sugar cane
and rattled in his trap* down to the harbour town   small cart
to sell his meat. He was a butcher.
Six-foot-three and very neat: high collar,
winged, a grey cravat, a waistcoat, watch-
chain just above the belt; thin narrow-
bottomed trousers, and the shoes his wife
would polish every night. He drove the trap
himself: slap of the leather reins
along the horse's back and he'd be off
with a top-hearted homburg* on his head: hat
black English country gentleman.

Now he is dead. The meat shop burned,
his property divided. A doctor bought
the horse. His mad alsatians killed it.
The wooden trap was chipped and chopped
by friends and neighbours and used to stop-
gap fences and for firewood. One yellow
wheel was rolled across the former cowpen gate.
Only his hat is left. I 'borrowed' it.
I used to try it on and hear the night wind
man go battering through the canes, cocks waking up and
    thinking
it was dawn throughout the clinking country night.
Great caterpillar tractors clatter down
the broken highway now; a diesel engine grunts
where pigs once hunted garbage.
A thin asthmatic* cow shares the untrashed garage.   breathes with difficulty

Edward Brathwaite

GROWING UP

Childhood

Long time he lay upon the sunny hill,
    To his father's house below securely bound.
Far off the silent, changing sound* was still,   passage of water
    With the black islands* lying thick around.   Orkney Islands north
                                                             of Scotland

He saw each separate height, each vaguer hue,
    Where the massed islands rolled in mist away,
And though all ran together in his view
    He knew that unseen straits between them lay.

Often he wondered what new shores were there.
    In thought he saw the still light on the sand,
The shallow water clear in tranquil* air   calm
    And walked through it in joy from strand to strand.

Over the sound a ship so slow would pass
    That in the black hill's gloom it seemed to lie.
The evening sound was smooth like sunken glass,
    And time seemed finished ere the ship passed by.

Grey tiny rocks slept round him where he lay,
    Moveless as they, more still as evening came,
The grasses threw straight shadows far away,
    And from the house his mother called his name.

Edwin Muir

Blue Girls

Twirling your blue skirts, travelling the sward*   walking on the lawns
Under the towers of your seminary*,   girl's school
Go listen to your teachers old and contrary
Without believing a word.

Tie the white fillets* then about your hair   headbands
And think no more of what will come to pass
Than bluebirds that go walking on the grass
And chattering on the air.

Practise your beauty, blue girls, before it fail;
And I will cry with my loud lips and publish
Beauty which all our power shall never establish*,   keep from decay
It is so frail.

For I could tell you a story which is true;
I know a woman with a terrible tongue,
Blear* eyes fallen from blue,   dull
All her perfections tarnished* – yet it is not long   spoilt
Since she was lovelier than any of you.

John Crowe Ransom

Teens

That was always my place, preferably
   at dusk, in a slight rain
– below the drenched allotment bank,
   by the bridge not often shaken by a train.

The neat hedge ended there, the fields began,
   sloping to shrouded hills,
and the lane grew pot-holed, led only
   to flowery pastures and abandoned mills.

There I would stand in the mizzle*, watching
   thirty martins or so
hawking silently above the meadows,
   high on black lines of flight, eerily low

             misty drizzle

as the heads of the grasses, swerving
   only at solid hedge
and me, a contentedly brooding phantom,
   at the lane's, at the night's, edge.

Molly Holden

A Song in the Front Yard

I've stayed in the front yard all my life.
I want a peek at the back
Where it's rough and untended and hungry weed grows.
A girl gets sick of a rose.

I want to go in the back yard now
And maybe down the alley,
To where the charity children play.
I want a good time today.

They do some wonderful things.
They have some wonderful fun.
My mother sneers, but I say it's fine
How they don't have to go in at quarter to nine.
My mother, she tells me that Johnnie Mae
Will grow up to be a bad woman.
That George'll be taken to Jail soon or late
(On account of last winter he sold our back gate).

But I say it's fine. Honest, I do.
And I'd like to be a bad woman, too,
And wear the brave stockings of night-black lace
And strut down the streets with paint on my face.

Gwendolyn Brooks

Suburban Eden

Booting a ball about, white shirtsleeves pumping
vivid on the summer dusk until beyond
the trees red car-lights came flickering on
and the corner garage burned violet,

or in winter shouting for reassurance
in mist's stillness with black boughs dripping
it could be miles from any house,

or just to sit on the shelter-bench staring out
at foliage darkening on darkening sky
till the pattern sparked live fire upon the brain,

doing was being. We grew,
sprawled balancing the sun on a nonchalant* knee,   not caring
and yes, there came girls elusive as water
awakening sharper pains, yet still in a world
sealed by the sky's rim round the park's edges,

unaware to the last: to the day
the train shook us down surprised in a gloomy terminus
fallen from lives rooted elsewhere, to pass
through the barrier clutching our season tickets.

And one can never go back.
Only to look: it is still going on,
on a frail rectangle of grass shaken out
where cloud-shadows pass boys are chasing a ball about,
girls call from the benches, the ball hangs
in the same arc over the same bough,
the foot aches to kick, held by fear
as of breaking glass.

As beyond the railings, the Addiscombe* train slides past,   South London suburb
dusty green, for the city; not yet for them.

Andrew Waterman

What has happened to Lulu?

What has happened to Lulu, mother?
    What has happened to Lu?
There's nothing in her bed but an old rag-doll
    And by its side a shoe.

Why is her window wide, mother,
    The curtain flapping free,
And only a circle on the dusty shelf
    Where her money-box used to be?

Why do you turn your head, mother,
    And why do the tear-drops fall?
And why do you crumple that note on the fire
    And say it is nothing at all?

I woke to voices late last night,
   I heard an engine roar.
Why do you tell me the things I heard
   Were a dream and nothing more?

I heard somebody cry, mother,
   In anger or in pain,
But now I ask you why, mother,
   You say it was a gust of rain.

Why do you wander about as though
   You don't know what to do?
What has happened to Lulu, mother?
   What has happened to Lu?

Charles Causley

Our Pale Daughters

When our pale daughters move in lamplight
Their long hair, black or golden, flows
And waterfalls on shoulders, eyes

Contemplate a time and place
That never was nor will be, whose
Trees bear bells and dreams of veils.

But when our daughters move in daylight,
Their locks* damned up in scarves, they see   hair
No trees or white lace in their street

But prams and dustbins, stubbled chins,
And hear cold choristers* with lungs   singers
Of steel singing of piston-rings.

Vernon Scannell

GROWING OLD

Good

The old man comes out on the hill
and looks down to recall earlier days
in the valley. He sees the stream shine,
the church stand, hears the litter of
children's voices. A chill in the flesh
tells him that death is not far off
now: it is the shadow under the great boughs
of life. His garden has herbs growing.
The kestrel goes by with fresh prey
in its claws. The wind scatters the scent
of wild beans. The tractor operates
on the earth's body. His grandson is there
ploughing; his young wife fetches him
cakes and tea and a dark smile. It is well.

R. S. Thomas

Childhood

I used to think that grown-up people chose
To have stiff backs and wrinkles round their nose,
And veins like small fat snakes on either hand,
On purpose to be grand.
Till through the banisters I watched one day
My great-aunt Etty's friend who was going away,
And how her onyx* beads had come unstrung.   a semi-precious stone
I saw her grope to find them as they rolled;
And then I knew that she was helplessly old,
As I was helplessly young.

Frances Cornford

To an Infant Grandchild

Dear Katherine, your future
Can never meet my past.
So short our common frontier,
Our hinterlands* so vast.

remote districts beyond
the frontier

Yet at the customs post
Light airs pass freely over
And all we need to know
We know of one another.

Though day will wake your country
As dark flows over mine
Your outback sleeps in shadow now.
Your smile is cloudless dawn.

E. J. Scovell

On Platform 5

I watch you gripping your hands
that have grown into the familiar contours
of old age, waiting for the train
to begin its terrifying journey
back to yourself, to your small house
where the daily habit of being alone
will have to be learnt all over again.

Whatever you do with your lined face
nothing disguises that look in your eyes.
Between you and your family
words push like passengers until
your daughter kisses you goodbye –
uttering those parting platitudes*
that spill about the closing of a door.

commonplace remarks

For them your visit's over and relief
jerks in the hands half-lifted now to wave.
Soon there will be far distances between
and duty letters counting out your year.
A whistle blows. The station moves away.
A magazine stays clenched upon your lap.
And your white knuckles tighten round each fear.

Edward Storey

He was

a brown old man with a green thumb:
I can remember the screak on stones of his hoe,
The chug, choke, and high madrigal* wheeze   squeaking
Of the spray-cart bumping below
The sputtery leaves of the apple trees,
But he was all but dumb

Who filled some quarter of the day with sound
All of my childhood long. For all I heard
Of his labours, I can now recall
Never a single word
Until he went in the dead of fall*   autumn
To the drowsy underground,

Having planted a young orchard with so great care
In that last year that none was lost, and May
Aroused them all, the leaves saying the land's
Praise for the livening clay,
And the found voice of his buried hands
Rose in the sparrowy air.

Richard Wilbur

Death in the Village

All afternoon she held her vague dark eyes
Bent to the window where an apple tree
Dandled* its fruit and leant against the pane;   danced
And it was through a drift of tangled leaves
That the two children she had never had
Ran home from school and whispered in the lane.

At four o'clock the husband she had not loved
Trudged round the corner, lifted up the latch
And through the slanting door let in the gold;
Turning her head she felt the chill strong breath,
And even as she waited for the kiss
Saw on his sleeve the grey churchyard mould.

And then the kettle sang, and as she stepped
Towards the kitchen threshold, there were two
Who many a year ago had courted her;
And she had not been kind; but there they were
Come back again, one brown with blazing eyes,
The other pale with seaweed in his hair.

A dear disorder stirred the ordered place
As all at once their voices filled the room
And dipped and circled in the air above her,
And chimed and sang and beat the silence back
In one accord, past all contention* now,   conflict
Treble and bass*, husband and child and lover.   high and low voiced

She had not time to ask why they had come,
For all the voices seemed to speak one thought.
'We waited long,' they said. 'Now you are free
To come with us.' And as they crowded round,
Smiling and calm, they held her and were gone,
Before she even thought to make the tea.

The kettle hissed alone and soon burned dry;
The clock struck five; the fire died. It was years
Since kin or company had crossed the floor.
Only the cat picked out with mincing* feet   walking delicately
His delicate way among the carpet flowers;
And all the rippled quiet lay smooth once more.

Graham Hough

NOTES AND
SUGGESTIONS FOR WORK

▷ : Topic for imaginative writing arising from ideas in the poem.

CHILDREN AND PARENTS

Morning Song　*Sylvia Plath*　108

The poet writes about her first feelings after the birth of her child. She cuts through conventional, cosy images of motherhood to tell, in unexpected terms, of the strangeness and mystery of her contact with the new born.

What impression is created in the first two verses? Look at the images which the poet uses. The naked, new child *shadows our safety*: it makes an older generation feel nearer death.

In the third verse, the mother speaks of the gulf she feels between her and her child. The mother is the cloud, the child is a pool of rainwater that the cloud has produced. Despite the reflection of the cloud in the puddle, there is really a vast gulf between them.

The last verses describe the mother listening to the child at night. Why say *moth breath*? Where are the roses? What does the baby remind her of as it cries? To what does she compare the sounds it makes?

Contrast the ideas presented here with the conventional picture of motherhood.

Children's Song　*R. S. Thomas*　109

The poet writes about childhood from the child's viewpoint. Adults try to understand childhood but cannot. How are adults portrayed in the poem? How do they try to enter the child's world? Which lines express the poet's disapproval of them? Which describe the secret magic of childhood?

The poet concludes with two images of a closed flower and blue eggs in a nest. How are the two ideas related? How do they both connect to the child/adult theme?

Janet Waking　*John Crowe Ransom*　109

How old is Janet, do you suppose, and how is she described? How exactly did Chucky die? Which phrases make the death seem humorous to us? What does Janet ask the adults to do about her pet? Explain the reference in the lines: *crying her brown hen/To rise and walk*. What cannot Janet understand about the death? How is death described in the grim last lines? Whose viewpoint is this?

For a similar poem about a child's inability to grasp the idea of death, see Wordsworth's *We are Seven*:

A simple child
That lightly draws its breath,
And feels its life in every limb,
What should it know of death?

For Cathy, on going to turn out her light   *Brian Jones*   110

Brian Jones compares his daughter's childish vision with his own adult imagination. He goes to his little daughter's room at night to check that she is all right. How does he feel as he enters? The room is full of examples of her imaginative play. What particular things has she been making and playing that day? What are the strangest or most amusing of these?

He concludes by considering his own dreams and imaginings. How are they different from Cathy's? How, in sleep, does her imaginative play continue?

Discord in Childhood   *D. H. Lawrence*   111

In his autobiographical novel, *Sons and Lovers*, Lawrence vividly describes an unhappy family incident. 'A huge old ash tree' in front of the house caught the full force of the wind sweeping across the valley:

> The tree shrieked again. . . To Paul it became almost a demoniacal noise. . . Having such a great space in front of the house gave the children a feeling of night, of vastness, and of terror. This terror came in from the shrieking of the tree and the anguish of the home discord. Often Paul would wake up. . . Then he heard the booming shouts of his father, come home nearly drunk, then the sharp replies of his mother. . . And then the whole was drowned in a piercing medley of shrieks and cries from the great, wind-swept ash-tree. . . There was a feeling of horror, a kind of bristling in the darkness, and a sense of blood.

The poem selects and sharpens this episode from the novel. The imagery is one addition: how is the violence of the tree and that of the parents related through the image of whips? What do the mother's *sharp replies* and the father's *booming shouts* become in the poem? What happened downstairs as a result of the quarrel? What is the tree a symbol of in this poem?

▷ : Write some scenes for a play called 'Discord in the Home'.

Fern Hill   *Dylan Thomas*   111

As a child, Dylan Thomas spent holidays at his uncle and aunt's remote Welsh farm, Fernhill. In his story *The Peaches*, he describes the shabby reality of the place:

> There was nowhere like that farmyard in all the slapdash county, nowhere so poor and grand and dirty as that square of mud and rubbish and bad wood and falling stone.

The poem gives a very different picture; it is less about a place than about a stage of life, or state of mind. Thomas builds a memory picture of childhood and youth, shown as a period of freshness, vitality and innocence. It is a flowing sketch of the child's observations, freedom, movement and feelings.

Pick out words and phrases which describe these.

Look carefully at the language in the poem. There are surprise phrases (*once below a time*), and invented adjectives (*lambwhite, househigh, whinnying green*). Find other examples of unusual language use. What is its effect upon the poem?

How is time seen in the poem? Follow the references to time that build into a major theme.

▷: Write about a place you knew as a child. Try to remember your feelings connected with that place.

Carrickfergus   *Louis Macneice*   113

Macneice tells of his earliest memories. He describes his boyhood in Northern Ireland, to the time when he crossed to England to attend boarding school.

He chooses precise details of things that seemed colourful, curious, or frightening to his childish eye or ear. What sights and sounds does he connect with Belfast? How did his father's position as a Protestant clergyman colour his memories and first ideas of social distinction?

The First World War looms large in his young experience. What details of sight, sound and smell does he remember from 1914–18?

How did his life seem to change when he went to boarding school? Why did school seem *a puppet world*, in contrast with what he had experienced before?

Rough   *Stephen Spender*   115

Stephen Spender describes the gulf between his own comfortable middle-class upbringing and the life of poor, tough boys in his district.

What were these boys like in appearance and behaviour? What did they do to Stephen? What images are connected with them? How are words *like stones*? Why should the pointing of the boys be described as *salt*? (Think how salt affects a wound.)

In what ways did Stephen fear them and in what ways did he admire them in their activities? *My world* sums up Stephen's way of life as a child. What features of his life would this include?

Which phrases suggest the boy's religious upbringing? What is the point of the last line? How did his parents try to protect Stephen? Were they right or wrong?

▷: 'The bullies': a story.

My Mother   *Claude McKay*   115

The poet's story of his mother's death is set in rural Jamaica.

What was the boy doing on the day of his mother's death? Why was he reluctant to leave her? What are his last memories of her in life? How did he hear the news of her death? What was his reaction?

What is the theme of the second verse, which portrays island life after the funeral?

Digging   *Seamus Heaney*   117
As he writes indoors, Heaney hears his father digging in the garden outside. He thinks back twenty years to his boyhood, when he used to admire his father's skill with a spade during the potato harvest. Which words convey the skill of the father's digging? His grandfather was also a craftsman with a spade. In what work did he show his skill?

Heaney cannot match the physical skills of previous generations of his family. What skill does he practise himself? What tool does he use instead of a spade? What image suggests its power?

Which lines in the poem (especially those recreating the feel and sound of farm work) demonstrate his particular skill?

▷ : Describe the skills that you admire in members of your family.

Long Distance   *Tony Harrison*   118
Harrison thinks lovingly of his parents, especially his father, who could never get used to being a widower.

What various things did the father do to pretend that his wife was still alive? What did he do when his son came to visit him? What did father fear that his son might say to him?

How does the son differ from his father? Yet, in the last two lines, what does the son imitate from his father's behaviour? What do you learn about human nature from this poem?

I was not there   *Karen Gershon*   119
Karen Gershon now lives in Israel. As a child she was saved from the Nazis in Germany, where Jews were brutally persecuted in the 1930s and 40s. Her parents remained behind and perished in concentration camps.

This poem is about her dead parents. *They set out from home*: where were they going? Why were they *relieved that it had come*? What does she find hard to imagine about her parents? What is the poet's chief regret about them now? What arguments does she present for and against this? Why does she feel guilty about them?

The poet writes in a strange, bleak way, without punctuation. The repetitions are effective – not only of the key theme – *I was not there to comfort them*, but also in the phrase *it is not true*, which suggests that she is trying hard to be exact and honest in her consideration of the past.

from Autobiography   *Adrian Henri*   120
Adrian Henri was brought up in Birkenhead, near Liverpool. He recalls his early memories with loving detail. Which words and images describe the liveliness and colour of the city, still a thriving Atlantic port in the 1930s?

His memories are dominated by family relationships, especially those with his grandparents. What were Grandad and Grandma like? What does he remember with affection (and sometimes fear) about them and their home?

Which details suggest the order and loving care they gave to their house and allotment?

In section three, the poet revisits the district. What has happened to his grandparents? What has changed about their house and district? Which words carry the poet's distaste for these changes?

What is the force of the last section of the poem, especially the next to last line?

▷: Write a careful portrait of your grandparents and their home.

from Ancestors   *Edward Brathwaite*   122
Braithwaite looks back on his childhood in Barbados. He remembers his grandfather, whom he loved and admired.

What qualities did he admire in his grandfather? How did the old man's appearance and costume reflect his pride in himself and his work?

The poet thinks sadly of the changes in his grandfather's property since his death. What are these? What is left? Which words and phrases in the last four lines suggest that life in Barbados seems to have grown harsher and more unpleasant since his grandfather's day?

Compare the details and theme of this poem with Adrian Henri's *Autobiography* (p. 120).

GROWING UP

Childhood   *Edwin Muir*   123
Muir remembers his boyhood on the Isle of Wyre, in the Orkneys, north of Scotland, in the late nineteenth century. Near his father's farm was a hill called the 'Castle'; he 'would sit there for hours in the summer evenings looking across the sound'.

The centre of the boy's world is still his home: he is *to his father's house below securely bound*. He returns to it each evening when *from the house his mother called his name*. However, the immense view from the hill, with its *unseen straits*, *new shores* and passing ships, fascinates him. It seemed to him like a map of the exciting mystery of his future life, when he will leave home and explore the world. Which words suggest the pleasure and excitement of this possible future?

Blue Girls   *John Crowe Ransom*   124
The American poet, John Crowe Ransom, watches young girls walking on the lawns of a boarding school. He sees their youth and beauty as touchingly short-lived. He advises them to ignore their teachers and to live in free enjoyment. What image is included in this advice? Time will soon take away their youth: what dreadful example does he hold before them?

Teens   *Molly Holden*   125

Molly Holden recalls a landscape that she relished as a teenager. To most people it would be unattractive, but to her it was full of atmosphere. It was a faithful mirror of her serious, reflective moods as an adolescent when she stood alone in the rain, watching. She identified the scene with something within herself.

What does *always* tell you about the place? What were the attractive and unattractive features that the girl loved in this scene? How does she describe herself here?

▷ : Your own chosen landscape – ugly or beautiful, in town or country – that reflects your feelings and with which you have some strong association.

A Song in the Front Yard   *Gwendolyn Brooks*   125

The *front yard* is the American equivalent of the English safe, protected back garden. How does being in the front yard sum up the girl's life until now? What does she long to do? Why does she want to mix with poorer, rougher young people? What does her mother think of this? Which details do you find comic or vivid in this poem?

▷ : Write a story called 'The young rebel'.

Suburban Eden   *Andrew Waterman*   126

The poet recalls a suburban park, where he used to go during his teenage years.

What were some of the games and activities that the boys enjoyed in the park? Which details of things he saw there create the atmosphere he remembers? What does he mean by *doing was being*? Which ideas in the poem suggest that he saw the park as his Garden of Eden?

What happens to the boys in the last three verses of the poem? The *barrier* and the *season tickets* are part of suburban railway commuting life: what else do they suggest about the boys' future lives? Which lines sum up their regret as they watch the park from the train?

What has happened to Lulu?   *Charles Causley*   127

The young child is puzzled about where Lulu, his elder sister, has gone. The child observes a series of clues which it cannot understand but which an older person can easily interpret.

Trace the various clues. What *has* happened to Lulu? What are the mother's feelings about the events of the night?

▷ : The story behind the poem, told by Lulu or the mother.

Our Pale Daughters   *Vernon Scannell*   128

Scannell contrasts dreams and reality in the lives of teenage girls.

The first two verses create an evening mood, where daydreams seem powerful. What are the girls dreaming of? What image describes the girls' appearance?

The last two verses are set in unromantic daytime. How are the girls changed in appearance by day? What do they see in the actual world around them? What do these things tell us about the girls' futures? How are men portrayed in the last section? Why is this portrayal so harsh?

What general comment on life and growing up is the poet making?

GROWING OLD

Good   *R. S. Thomas*   129

The Welsh clergyman poet, R. S. Thomas, here sees old age as a time of fulfilment and confidence in the richness and continuity of life.

As the old man contemplates his home valley, he is aware of three things. What are these and what do they represent generally about a man's life? How is he aware of coming death? What image is used to describe it? What other pictures of continuing life are used? How does he feel about the work and the marriage of his grandson? What does the sentence *It is well* suggest?

Compare with the poem *Gardening Sunday* by Brian Jones (p. 96).

▷ : An old person looks back on his or her life.

Childhood   *Frances Cornford*   129

The poet recalls an incident from her childhood that made her suddenly appreciate what is pitiful in old people. How had she seen the elderly before this? What was the incident itself? What did the girl learn from it?

What double meaning does the title have?

To an Infant Grandchild   *E. J. Scovell*   130

Relations between grandparent and grandchild often have a peculiar tenderness. Yet there is a strangeness about them too: the one has a lifetime's experience; the other a lifetime to come. The poet considers her own grandchild, Katherine, in this light.

In a series of delicate images, she compares their two lives to two countries. One country is her own past; the other the child's future. Their frontier is their present shared relationship. There is no barrier, no *customs post* between them: they exchange affection as easily as breezes blow across a national frontier. How is the imagery continued in the last verse?

▷ : A portrait of a well-loved grandparent or elderly person you know well.

On Platform 5   *Edward Storey*   130

On a railway station, Storey watches an elderly traveller returning home after staying with his/her married daughter.

Which words and phrases express his/her anxiety and tension? The train journey will lead *back to yourself*: what does this mean? How does the old person's family behave at the station? What is the poet's attitude to the family?

▷: *Either*, the old person's life at home: his or her thoughts, activities and anxieties. *Or*, his or her feelings as he/she says goodbye and travels back to an empty house.

He was   *Richard Wilbur*   131
Richard Wilbur remembers an old gardener whom he knew as a child. (To have a *green thumb* means that you are good at gardening.)

Where did the man work? What does Wilbur recall about him? He sees the man almost as some spirit of nature, who dies in autumn and comes alive in spring, in the form of the orchard that he planted. The new growth in the trees seems to come from his *livening clay*, – the vitality coming from the old man's dead body underground. He never said much in life: how does he find expression after death?

Death in the Village   *Graham Hough*   132
The thoughts of an old woman on the last afternoon of her life. She ponders the important relationships of her life, real and imagined. The people involved appear to her like ghosts. What are these various relationships and what is strange or sad about them? Notice the importance of the negative words in the first three verses. Why, particularly, does one man have seaweed in his hair? *In one accord, past all contention now*: what has happened to the woman's relationships as she nears death?

Smiling and calm, they held her and were gone: do you find this picture of death comforting or distressing? How is the woman's loneliness made clear in the last verse?

The poem has a very delicate, quiet atmosphere. Pick out some words and phrases, especially in the first and last verses, that create this.

▷: Write a story about the woman and any of her relationships.

GENERAL QUESTIONS

1. Which of the autobiographical poems did you find most interesting in the 'Children and parents' section?
2. What do these poems tell us about *either* the difficulties of parent/child relationships *or* the pleasure and problems of adolescence?
3. What do the poets find impressive or pathetic about old age?
4. Which writers in this section do you think show most sympathy and feeling for their subjects?

REFLECTIONS
AND IMAGININGS

REFLECTIONS

What then?

His chosen comrades thought at school
He must grow a famous man;
He thought the same and lived by rule,
All his twenties crammed with toil;
'What then?' sang Plato's* ghost. 'What then?'   a Greek thinker

Everything he wrote was read,
After certain years he won
Sufficent money for his need,
Friends that have been friends indeed;
'What then?' sang Plato's ghost. 'What then?'

All his happier dreams came true –
A small old house, wife, daughter, son,
Grounds where plum and cabbage grew,
Poets and Wits* about him drew;   writers and thinkers
'What then?' sang Plato's ghost. 'What then?'

'The work is done,' grown old he thought,
'According to my boyish plan;
Let the fools rage, I swerved in naught*,   nothing
Something to perfection brought';
But louder sang that ghost, 'What then?'

W. B. Yeats

Happiness

I asked professors who teach the meaning of life to
    tell me what is happiness.
And I went to famous executives who boss the work of
    thousands of men.
They all shook their heads and gave me a smile as though
    I was trying to fool with them.
And then one Sunday afternoon I wandered out along the   in Chicago, U.S.A.
    Desplaines* river
And I saw a crowd of Hungarians under the trees with
    their women and children and a keg of beer and an
    accordian.

Carl Sandburg

Picnic on the Lawn

Their dresses were splashed on the green
Like big petals; polished spoons shone
And tinkered with cup and saucer.
Three women sat there together.

They were young, but no longer girls.
Above them the soft green applause
Of leaves acknowledged their laughter.
Their voices moved at a saunter*.   leisurely pace

Small children were playing nearby;
A swing hung from an apple tree
And there was a sand pit for digging.
Two of the picnicking women

Were mothers. The third was not.
She had once had a husband, but
He had gone to play the lover
With a new lead in a different theatre.

One of the mothers said, 'Have you
Cherished a dream, a fantasy
You know is impossible; a childish
Longing to do something wildly

'Out of character? I'll tell you mine.
I would like to drive alone
In a powerful sports car, wearing
A headscarf and dark glasses, looking

'Sexy and mysterious and rich.'
The second mother smiled: 'I wish
I could ride through an autumn morning
On a chestnut mare, cool wind blowing

'The jet black hair I never had
Like smoke streaming from my head,
In summer swoop on a switchback sea
Surf-riding in a black bikini.'

She then turned to the childless one:
'And you? You're free to make dreams true.
You have no need of fantasies
Like us domestic prisoners.'

A pause, and then the answer came:
'I also have a hopeless dream:
Tea on the lawn in a sunny garden,
Listening to the voices of my children.'

Vernon Scannell

Hay for the Horses

He had driven half the night
From far down San Joaquin*   in California, U.S.A.
Through Mariposa*, up the
Dangerous mountain roads,
And pulled in at eight a.m.
With his big truckload of hay
   behind the barn.
With winch and ropes and hooks
We stacked the bales up clean
To splintery redwood rafters
High in the dark, flecks of alfalfa*   animal fodder
Whirling through shingle-cracks of light,
Itch of haydust in the
   sweaty shirt and shoes.
At lunchtime under black oak
Out in the hot corral*,   pen for horses
– The old mare nosing lunchpails,
Grasshoppers crackling in the weeds –
'I'm sixty-eight,' he said,
'I first bucked hay when I was seventeen.
I thought, that day I started,
I sure would hate to do this all my life.
And dammit, that's just what
I've gone and done.'

Gary Snyder

The Road not Taken

Two roads diverged* in a yellow wood,   split into two directions
And sorry I could not travel both
And be one traveller, long I stood
And looked down one as far as I could
To where it bent in the undergrowth;

Then took the other, as just as fair,
And having perhaps the better claim,
Because it was grassy and wanted wear*;   was little used
Though as for that the passing there
Had worn them really about the same,

And both that morning equally lay
In leaves no step had trodden black.
Oh, I kept the first for another day!
Yet knowing how way leads on to way,
I doubted if I should ever come back.

I shall be telling this with a sigh
Somewhere ages and ages hence:
Two roads diverged in a wood, and I –
I took the one less travelled by,
And that has made all the difference.

Robert Frost

Outside

The towered church squats
among willows, dead elms and lindens
beside a deep pond nearly hid
in nettles, thistles, knapweed and briars.
The churchyard is bowered in weeds.
In one of its lost graves four children,
Belinda, Jane, Ivy and Tom
have lain more than a century.
Wild fairy flax is now their host.

The churchyard gate won't open.
How did those boys last week
find the place, climb the tower,
hurl a stone block down
on Belinda, Ivy, Tom and Jane,
push over an acanthus* urn   spike leaved plant
which showed above uncut grass?
Did the pond's echo and the neglect of the place
make them so spurn* reason?   reject

If this was not so, one can't quite think
why the boys slashed the unused altar,
broke a vase. No theft: moneyed pockets coveted
      nothing . . .
I cannot hate those heirs of our violence
our vandals. (Though no doubt I might
if I came face to face with them here.)
The church is locked, the altar flat.
Is it the boys, or we, who are shut out?
Or could it possibly be God? And from what?

Anne Tibble

In a Country Church

To one kneeling down no word came,
Only the wind's song, saddening the lips
Of the grave saints, rigid in glass;
Or the dry whisper of unseen wings,
Bats not angels, in the high roof.

Was he balked* by silence? He kneeled long,   disappointed
And saw love in dark crown
Of thorns blazing, and a winter tree
Golden with fruit of a man's body.

R. S. Thomas

Photograph of Haymaker, 1890

It is not so much the image of the man
that's moving – he pausing from his work
to whet* his scythe, trousers tied   sharpen
below the knee, white shirt lit by
another summer's sun, another century's –
as the sight of the grasses beyond
his last laid swathe*, so living yet   line of cut grass
upon the moment previous to death;
for as the man stooping straightened up
and bent again they died before his blade.

Sweet hay and gone some seventy years ago
and yet they stand before me in the sun,
stems damp still where their neighbours' fall
uncovered them, succulent* and straight,   thick and juicy
immediate with moon-daisies.

Molly Holden

Some Pictures of the Thirties

The stiff pages turn. Most of the photographs
Are faded now; the air the subjects breathe
Is grey, or amber like weak milkless tea;
A huddle of hunched streets, two cenotaphs*,   war memorials
Burglar's caps and scarves; hard to believe
The child I was lived there in 'thirty-three.

Sepia* or grey is what each print allows,   brown
Yet I recall cobbles swimming in gold
As, in blue shimmer, a nodding pony pulled
An ice-cream cart along the hollow street
As chopping paces slowly fell, dead bells
Of hooves that measured Sunday's ritual drowse.

Other Sundays, too: festive processions,
Float of embroidered banners*, ribbon-skirl,   *of churches or trades unions
Well-scrubbed boys, white ankle-socks of girls;
A kind of holiness in those occasions,
An innocence; the fragrance lingers still,
Drifts through the darkening archives of the skull.

But there were other walks, the long grey marches
In silence, save for a mouth-organ's starved wail,
Towards the specious* South of broken promises,   *good only in appearance
Past black, shut factories and frozen churches –
Hunger and shame with medals, a long, long trail
Into a darkness cold and without torches.

Turn the page quickly, brave faces of the Thirties:
Pale concentrated stares of bantamweights*,   *light weight boxers
Hair centre-parted, greased; their whippet bodies
Lean and white. There were few heavyweights
In British rings and none of them could fight.
Put away the pictures. Turn out the light.

But the flickering ghosts will not at once be quenched.
They stay and, with them, many sounds: laments,
Woodbine*-hoarse, for charred disasters – trains,   *cheap cigarettes
Dirigibles*, bi-planes – and those other musics,   *airships
The clang of trams, blunt chime of pony's hooves;
And then these fade. The past lies still, yet moves.

Vernon Scannell

Above Pate Valley

We finished clearing the last
Section of trail by noon,
High on the ridge-side
Two thousand feet above the creek –
Reached the pass, went on
Beyond the white pine groves,
Granite shoulders, to a small
Green meadow watered by the snow,
Edged with Aspen* – sun   a kind of tree
Straight high and blazing
But the air was cool.
Ate a cold fried trout in the
Trembling shadows. I spied
A glitter, and found a flake
Black volcanic glass – obsidian* –   dark, glass-like lava
By a flower. Hands and knees
Pushing the Bear grass, thousands
Of arrowhead leavings over a
Hundred yards. Not one good
Head, just razor flakes
On a hill snowed all but summer,
A land of fat summer deer,
They came to camp. On their
Own trails. I followed my own
Trail here. Picked up the cold-drill,
Pick, singlejack*, and sack   a tool
Of dynamite.
Ten thousand years.

Gary Snyder

Dinosaurs

One idly reads: 'Tyrannosaurus rex,
The greatest of carnivorous* dinosaurs.'   flesh-eating
At once a curious opening of doors;
Both time-scale and the usual scene perplex.
There was a history when I wasn't here,
Perhaps a similar period to come;
But how amazing that the huge and dumb
Could dominate this all-familiar sphere*.   scene of daily life

My being master of the world's as odd
As having lived a freeish citizen.
Contemporaneous* with the louse and cod,   living at the same time
We never count our blessings;
                              now and then,
Indeed, hear through the noisy wars of men
Time whisper to the rodent*: Be a god.   rat

Roy Fuller

During Wind and Rain

They sing their dearest songs –
He, she, all of them – yea,
Treble and tenor and bass*,   high and low voices
    And one to play;
With the candles mooning* each face. . . .   lighting up the side of
    Ah, no; the years O!   each face
How the sick leaves reel* down in throngs!   spin

They clear the creeping moss –
Elders and juniors – aye,
Making the pathways neat
    And the garden gay;
And they build a shady seat. . .
    Ah, no; the years, the years;
See, the white storm-birds wing across.

They are blithely* breakfasting all –   happily
Men and maidens – yea,
Under the summer tree,
    With a glimpse of the bay
While pet fowl come to the knee. . .
    Ah, no; the years O!
And the rotten rose is ript from the wall.

They change to a high new house,
He, she, all of them – aye,
Clocks and carpets and chairs
    On the lawn all day,
And brightest things that are theirs. . .
    Ah, no; the years, the years;
Down their carved names the rain-drop ploughs.

Thomas Hardy

Working Girls

The working girls in the morning are going to work – long
    lines of them afoot amid the downtown stores and
    factories, thousands with little brick-shaped lunches
    wrapped in newspapers under their arms.
Each morning as I move through this river of young woman
    life I feel a wonder about where it is all going, so many
    with a peach blossom of young years on them and
    laughter of red lips and memories in their eyes of dances
    the night before and plays and walks.

Green and grey streams side by side in a river and so here
    are always the others, those who have been over the
    way, the women who know each one the end of life's
    gamble for her, the meaning and the clue, the how and
    the why of the dances and the arms that passed around
    their waists and the fingers that played in their hair.
Faces go by written over: 'I know it all, I know where the
    bloom and the laughter go and I have memories,' and
    the feet of these move slower and they have wisdom
    where the others have beauty.
So the green and the grey move in the early morning on the
    downtown streets.

Carl Sandburg

The Three O'clock Shift

The buzzer awakes me, and shortly I hear
The three o'clock shift down the road come clattering:
The noise of their tackety* boots ringing clear   hob-nailed
On the frozen metal, and the young lads chattering,
And whistling and singing, as they go by,
To the undimmed stars of the icy sky.

They pass the house; and I turn in my bed
To slumber again; but the tacketies' clattering
Still rings in my brain, and still in my head
The singing of youth and the whistling and chattering –
Of youth that whistles and sings for a bit
To the winter stars on the way to the pit.

Wilfrid Gibson

Labour Exchange

These men, clutching cards, stand in slack groups
Round the stove in the wooden room, fog
Shoving its dim nose around the door.

The clock keeps a prim eye on them, intent
On supervision, and white with disapproval of
Their profane disillusion and their thick mirth.

They have had a slice of bread and lard;
Warmed their hands at a cup of tea;
Left wives scrubbing in aprons of sacking,

For this, the terminus* of hopes and sorrows,   final point
Where the blazing stadium and the satisfaction of food,
Or the cipher* of want, daily arrive and depart.   nothingness

They stand for many hours, obscure,
Glimpsing through windows the autumn sun on
The spires of the world they built, but do not share.

Clifford Dyment

The Explosion

On the day of the explosion
Shadows pointed towards the pithead:
In the sun the slagheap slept.

Down the lane came men in pitboots
Coughing oath-edged talk and pipe-smoke,
Shouldering off the freshened silence.

One chased after rabbits; lost them;
Came back with a nest of lark's eggs;
Showed them; lodged them in the grasses.

So they passed in beards and moleskins*,   miners' trousers
Fathers, brothers, nicknames, laughter,
Through the tall gates standing open.

At noon, there came a tremor; cows
Stopped chewing for a second; sun,
Scarfed as in a heat-haze, dimmed.

The dead go on before us, they
Are sitting in God's house in comfort,
We shall see them face to face –

Plain as lettering in the chapels
It was said, and for a second
Wives saw men of the explosion

Larger than in life they managed –
Gold as on a coin, or walking
Somehow from the sun towards them,

One showing the eggs unbroken.

Philip Larkin

When I heard the learn'd astronomer

When I heard the learn'd astronomer,
When the proofs, the figures, were ranged in columns before
    me,
When I was shown the charts and diagrams, to add, divide,
    and measure them,
When I sitting heard the astronomer where he lectured with
    much applause in the lecture-room,
How soon unaccountable I became tired and sick,
Till rising and gliding out I wander'd off by myself,
In the mystical moist night-air, and from time to time,
Look'd up in perfect silence at the stars.

Walt Whitman

The Fox

'In the evening we reached the island of San Pedro, where
we found the *Beagle* at anchor. In doubling the point, two of
the officers landed to take a round of angles with the
theodolite. A fox (Canis fulvipes) of a kind said to be
peculiar to the island, and very rare in it, and which is a
new species, was sitting on the rocks. He was so intently
absorbed in watching the work of the officers, that I was
able, by quietly walking up behind, to knock him on the
head with my geological hammer.'

Charles Darwin *Voyage of the Beagle*

On the stone island, rough with rocks,
Tawny* among the grey, a fox   brownish-yellow
Sat. Round his haunches the brush curled
Demurely* as a pennant* furled,   neatly   flag
Signal of peace and self-won ease.
The spearflight of a wedge* of geese   V-formation
Hardly disturbed his sleekness, still
As a small cloud on a smooth hill,
Resting half-anchored. Then a shout
From the dull water echoes out.
He cocks an ear; his other sense
Through nose and eye gains evidence
Of movement on the shore. Some men,
Their boat dragged high, sea-booted, kin
To nothing on this desolate coast,
Stand earnestly about a post
Three-legged to their two. They probe,
And stoop, and peer along a tube*   the theodolite
With purposeless intensity.
The fox cranes out his neck to see
What hunting or what play is this,
When from his back, descending hiss,
The hammer falls. A twitch, a leap,
The golden flanks are dead asleep
For ever, the inquisitive eye
Starting and glazed to eternity,

And Mr Darwin, with a cough,
Scoops up the body and makes off,
Dangling another link to show
The fine mesh* of his theory. So   complicated structure
Dies the live fox. The living man
Somehow will prove this nature's plan,
Selected by his larger skull
To crack the other. Pitiful
And far away the whole affair,
Yet breeding all dilemma* there.   agonising problems
The animals of science have
Invaded life. The wise and brave
Are nothing or corrupted. Now
The mushroom cloud* begins to grow.   the atomic bomb

Robert Gittings

Open Day at Porton

These bottles are being filled with madness,
A kind of liquid madness concentrate
Which can be drooled across the land
Leaving behind a shuddering human highway. . .

   A welder trying to eat his arm.

   Children pushing stale food into their eyes
   To try to stop the chemical spectaculars
   Pulsating inside their hardening skulls.

   A health visitor throwing herself downstairs,
   Climbing the stairs, throwing herself down again
   Shouting: Take the nails out of my head.

There is no damage to property.

Now, nobody likes manufacturing madness,
But if we didn't make madness in bottles
We wouldn't know how to deal with bottled madness.

We don't know how to deal with bottled madness.

We all really hate manufacturing madness
But if we didn't make madness in bottles
We wouldn't know how to be sane.

Responsible madness experts assure us
Britain would never be the first
To uncork such a global brainquake.

But suppose some foreign nut sprayed Kent
With his insanity aerosol. . .
Well, there's only one answer to madness.

Adrian Mitchell

Mrs. Middleditch

Fitting a thin glove
Over a dry hand,
Over a gold ring (plain
As the nine-carat love
Of her good man now dead),
Mrs Middleditch pats
For the sake of tidiness
The back of her tidy head.

'It's time for shopping again.
I must think of the things I need,
Or *think* I need. Time
To go out. If I stay in
I mightn't go out at all.
I might give way to doubt
And ask, What *is* it all *for*?
And not go out of my door:

'And think, Why leave my bed
To wash and dress and eat,
And wash up, and wash out a dress,
And dress up, and go out to tea?
Sameness of fading days,
Is this what life should be?
Am I the slightest use?
And who would ever miss *me*?

'I must make out a list,
I suppose a widow must eat:
A caterpillar must eat –
But then, it can hope for wings.
Floor polish, cocoa cake,
Sago, margarine, yeast –
A gruesome menu there
For my lonesome evening feast!'

'Oh, Mrs. Middleditch, good
Morning to you!'
                                'And to you!'
'A lovely morning again!'
'It is. (But you give me a pain;
What goes on in my head
You neither care nor guess;
One can have a little too much
Bright neighbourliness.)'

At the Supermarket door
An amplifier hails
Each housewife – and her purse –
With smooth false bonhomie*.   friendliness
Could anything be worse?
Mrs. Middleditch hears
With a shiver of distaste
These words affront her ears:

'A Supermorning, madam,
For Supermarketing!
Our cut-price Superfoods
Are best for each and all,

Our Supergoods await you
On every Supershelf,
So take a Superbasket
And help your Superself!

'Oh, Mrs. Middleditch,
This place *is* a boon!
I've come here for everything
Since my honeymoon.'
'Yes, yes, convenient,
Marvellous, I agree –
And yet I feel somehow as if
It's pressing in on me:

'There's too much of everything,
Too much advertisement.
I ask myself if what is said
Is ever what is meant –
FISH FLAKES *taste breezy,*
CAKE FIX *bakes lightest,*
QUICK WAX *makes work easy,*
SQUELCH *whitens whites whitest.'*

'Oh, Mrs. Middleditch,
Excuse me if I ask it.
But you've not got a single thing
So far in your Superbasket!
Let me recommend these peaches
And the nice thick double cream,
And you'll find the chicken breasts
(Milk-fed, of course) a dream.'

'I've got a list of things I need
Or thought I needed. Now I know
That peaches, chickens, cream,
And even sago, cocoa, yeast,
Are things I cannot buy today.
Today I fast, not feast.
I can't put out my hand, I find
A double vision in my mind.

'Beyond abundance – butter, eggs,
Strength-giving meat and cubes of cheese,
And cylinders of beans and peas
And syrup-swimming halves of pears –
Deserts I see, and frowsty rags,
And groups of persons wearing these,
Bowed by the weight of nothingness;
I recognize them – refugees.

'I see a child with seething flies
Fouling its big, unblinking eyes,
Eyes fixed on me: a swollen child,
With dangling, thin, rachitic* wrists,   disease of malnutrition
Listless and silent, watching me,
In want and in unwantedness
Wanting to learn why it was born –
While I draw up my shopping lists.

'It will not do! I have no appetite
For food. And none for charity!
Dull, shiftless outcasts under static skies,
They are myself. Only the pelican
That tore her breast could teach me how
To reach that place, to staunch with work
That open sore, to feed with love
One orphan fed upon by flies.'

'Oh Mrs. Middleditch! Are you all right?'
Her answer was a sudden moan
And down she slumped upon the Superfloor,
The spotless floor of Non-Slip Superstone.
Inside her Superbasket was her head,
Unconscious prisoner of a Supercage.
'Quick, call the manager!' 'She was acting strange.'
'Silly old fool! She's reached the awkward age.'

William Plomer

Geography Lesson

When the jet sprang into the sky,
it was clear why the city
had developed the way it had,
seeing it scaled six inches to the mile.
There seemed an inevitability*   no other way of doing
about what on ground had looked haphazard*,   set out at random
unplanned and without style
when the jet sprang into the sky.

When the jet reached ten thousand feet,
it was clear why the country
had cities where rivers ran
and why the valleys were populated.
The logic of geography –
that land and water attracted man –
was clearly delineated*   marked out
when the jet reached ten thousand feet.

When the jet rose six miles high,
it was clear that the earth was round
and that it had more sea than land.
But it was difficult to understand
that the men on the earth found
causes to hate each other, to build
walls across cities and to kill.
From that height, it was not clear why.

Zulfikar Ghose

Happiness

Some say this is a golden age,
That never again
Will there be such a deal to eat,
Such space between the race of men.

My day's benign* routines incline   gentle
To such belief
However startling, since it's sure
In time (and more than likely brief)

One will awaken not to eggs,
And isolation
In gardens, but a bed of crowding
Visitors, and emaciation*.   leanness
                                                      (because of illness)

Roy Fuller

So that we build

In a great silence I hear approaching rain:
There is a sound of conflict in the sky.
The frightened lizard darts behind a stone.
First was the wind, now is the wild assault.

I wish this world would sink and drown again
So that we build another Noah's ark
And send another little dove to find
What we have lost in floods of misery.

Martin Carter

IMAGININGS

From the Domain of Arnheim

And so that all these ages, these years
we cast behind us, like the smoke-clouds
dragged back into vacancy when the rocket springs –

The domain of Arnheim was all snow, but we were there.
We saw a yellow light thrown on the icefield
from the huts by the pines, and laughter came up
floating from a white corrie*
miles away, clearly.
We moved on down, arm in arm.
I know you would have thought it was a dream
but we were there. And those were trumpets –
tremendous round the rocks –
while they were burning fires of trash and mammoths'
    bones.
They sang naked, and kissed in the smoke.
A child, or one of their animals, was crying.
Young men blew the ice crystals off their drums.
We came down among them, but of course
they could see nothing, on their time-scale.
Yet they sensed us, stopped, looked up – even into our eyes.
To them we were a displacement of the air,
a sudden chill, yet we had no power
over their fear. If one of them had been dying
he would have died. The crying
came from one just born: that was the cause
of the song. We saw it now. What had we stopped
but joy?
I know you felt
the same dismay, you gripped my arm, they were waiting
for what they knew of us to pass.

hollow on mountainside

A sweating trumpeter took
a brand from the fire with a shout and threw it
where our bodies would have been –
we felt nothing but his courage.
And so they would deal with every imagined power
seen or unseen.
There are no gods in the domain of Arnheim.

We signalled to the ship; got back;
our lives and days returned to us, but
haunted by deeper souvenirs than any rocks or seeds.
From time the souvenirs are deeds.

Edwin Morgan

Limbo[*]

place of oblivion

The air-gauge clamped our heartbeats. When we searched
the cabin – firm again, relentless – a
stir of limbs confirmed the needle's lurch.
How full of charm proved our young stowaway!

How to tell someone that his offence is mortal
merely in that the fuel his weight would cost, the air
he breathes, is more than one frail cosmic-ship can spare?
His grin said, *Company*! could not believe the portal

that leads to new worlds from this fetid* womb
must suck him forth to – limbo. Yet he went
quietly into the airlock. There's no room
for sentiment in space. We meant

stinking

him well enough. . . . Zoë, it's not our fault; you must
eat. We bear supplies for the living, put them first.

D. M. Thomas

A Dead Planet

1

The captain primed his crew, disconsolate*
Upon the bleak, the broken-pillared plain;

unhappy and disappointed

Waving a tentacle, he snapped. 'The State
Will want to know how primitive a brain

Presided here. We must *resuscitate*. . . .'
(A thrill bestirred their pinions*.) 'We trust the grain

bring back to life

wings

Of skull that Luth is working on was late
Enough in time for the blueprints to remain,

Enabling our machine to build – and wait
To see what kind of animate was slain

So summarily, as it appears; what fate
Extinguished it.' Deep silence then.

2

                              . . . The 'Man'
– Such was the thing called, till the desolate
Decade of falling rain,

The white-hot ash – was shrivelled, bifurcate*.
'*Master*!' his lips compounded while the skein*

forked (two legged)

blindness

Was falling from the eyes he had just shut
On wife, on child: his faith was not in vain!

'*Dear Christ*! . . . *how blissfully Thou dost abate
The grave's* –' His gaze took in the plain;

The ring of orbs* devoid of love or hate,
The ray-guns poised to mow it down again

large eyes

When they had sorted out its true estate.

D. M. Thomas

Missionary

A harsh entry I had of it, Grasud;
the tiny shuttle strained to its limits
by radiation-belts, dust-storms,
not to mention the pitiless heat which
hit it on plunging into the atmosphere
– its fire-shield clean vaporized; and then,
on landing, the utter cold and stillness
of a mountain-slope, cedar-trees and
what they call
snow. As I went numbly through the
routine I could do in my sleep –
mentalizing myself, smothering
my body and the shuttle in a
defensive neutrino-screen, hiding them
securely in the snow,
I looked up and, between the branches
of the cedars, could see
the mother-ship sliding away through
the dark, like an unfixed star, westwards
to its other destinations: that was
the worst moment of all, Grasud! I'd have
called it back! So lonely, such an alien
world they'd left me in. Goodbye, Lagash!
goodbye, Theremon! fare well! (But no
voice now even to make a gesture against
the silence.)
                Then the agonizingly slow
descent, towards the village,
my spirit dark, already missing
not only Theremon and Lagash, but
that other friend, my body's familiar
chemistry. By now I felt my
vaunted courage ebbing, Grasud; I think
those years of training
alone forced me to go on, into the village,

spoken by an alien from another part of the universe

into the houses, inns, into
– after much vain searching – a ripened
womb; there superseding*   took the place of
(not without a pang) its foetus-spirit.
How black that airlock,
after the six suns of our own system,
I needn't tell you. Even space,
in recollection, seemed a blaze of
supernovas*. But I settled to my task   very bright stars
wrestling to get on terms with carbon
compounds* fearsomely different from   that the human body is
the synthetic* ones I'd practised in.   made from
Of course, as I was born and the years   artificial
passed, it seemed as natural to go
on man's two legs as on our Vardian
limbs. But when these pains eased,
one far bitterer grew: my seeds were cast
on stony ground; the more
I exhorted,
– the more I spoke, obliquely* of   indirectly
the many mansions of our Vardian
Commonwealth, and of the place
that could be theirs – the more it
seemed those simple, instinctive creatures
lied, stole, slandered, fornicated,
killed. . . . Grasud, how often, sick with
failure, only the words of Vrak
sustained me – 'a world lies in your hands.'
That was the time he
sent for the three of us when
all ears were ringing with the news of
the three life-planets found in
NDT 1065. If we had hopes,
we masked them. His words to us, for
all that's happened, I'll hoard always.
'Thoorin, Lagash, Theremon,' I hear him
saying, 'I'm sending *you*. . . . you're young,
but this is what you've trained for, bio-
enlightenment. You've done well.'
And then – 'a world lies in your hands.'

So, Grasud, I toiled. In the end
I tried too hard; the time of space –
rendezvous* was almost come. Anyway   meeting place
they killed me. I loved them, and they
killed me.
       Yes, it was hard,
as you can well imagine,
on the return-journey, to avoid feeling
the faintest warp of
jealousy, as Theremon and
Lagash talked with
the happy emissaries* of their   ambassadors
planets. – What does Vrak say? He is
kind, promises – after this loathsome
rest – another
chance, though not of course on that
planet. My 'inability' (he avoids
the word failure) to raise them
ethically* to the point where we could   morally
safely announce ourselves, proves, he
says, there's no point trying again
for a few thousand years. Meanwhile,
he suggests, maybe some of my words
will start to bear fruit. . . . He is kind!
His last words were 'Forget about it,
Thoorin; enjoy your stay on
Atar.' Forget!
with the relaxed faces of my friends a
perpetual thorn!

D. M. Thomas

The Horses

Barely a twelvemonth after
The seven days war that put the world to sleep,
Late in the evening the strange horses came.
By then we had made our covenant* with silence,   terms
But in the first few days it was so still
We listened to our breathing and were afraid.
On the second day
The radios failed; we turned the knobs; no answer.
On the third day a warship passed us, heading north,
Dead bodies piled on the deck. On the sixth day
A plane plunged over us into the sea. Thereafter
Nothing. The radios dumb;
And still they stand in corners of our kitchens,
And stand, perhaps, turned on, in a million rooms
All over the world. But now if they should speak,
If on a sudden they should speak again,
If on the stroke of noon a voice should speak,
We would not listen, we would not let it bring
That old bad world that swallowed its children quick*   alive
At one great gulp. We would not have it again.
Sometimes we think of the nations lying asleep,
Curled blindly in impenetrable* sorrow,   cannot be penetrated
And then the thought confounds us with its strangeness.

The tractors lie about our fields; at evening
They look like dank sea-monsters couched and waiting.
We leave them where they are and let them rust:
'They'll moulder away and be like other loam*.   soil
We make our oxen drag our rusty ploughs,
Long laid aside. We have gone back
Far past our fathers' land
                              And then, that evening
Late in the summer the strange horses came.
We heard a distant tapping on the road,
A deepening drumming; it stopped, went on again.

And at the corner changed to hollow thunder.
We saw the heads
Like a wild wave charging and were afraid.
We had sold our horses in our fathers' time
To buy new tractors. Now they were strange to us
As fabulous steeds set on an ancient shield
Or illustrations in a book of knights.
We did not dare go near them. Yet they waited,
Stubborn and shy, as if they had been sent
By an old command to find our whereabouts
And that long-lost archaic* companionship.   out-of-date
In the first moment we had never thought
They they were creatures to be owned and used.
Among them were some half-a-dozen colts
Dropped in some wilderness of the broken world,
Yet new as if they had come from their own Eden.
Since then they have pulled our ploughs and borne our
      loads,
But that free servitude* still can pierce our hearts.   subjection to a master
Our life is changed; their coming our beginning.
Edwin Muir

NOTES AND
SUGGESTIONS FOR WORK

▷ : Topic for imaginative writing arising from ideas in the poem.

REFLECTIONS

What then?   *W. B. Yeats*   144

An account of the life of a successful writer, which resembles that of Yeats himself. What are the signs of his success? What is his attitude to that success?

Plato, the Greek thinker (427–347 B.C.), considered that there are ideal, spiritual forms of love and beauty, besides which human efforts should be measured. Why does his ghost taunt the writer, with the mocking *What then?* refrain? What do you think he means? What do you think is missing from the writer's life?

Happiness   *Carl Sandburg*   145

Sandburg asks various 'successful' people about their definitions of happiness. What are their answers?

A group of poor Hungarian immigrants, struggling to seek their fortune in Chicago, USA, gives him an answer. What are they doing? What kind of happiness is this? What comment does this poem make about other sorts of happiness?

Picnic on the Lawn   *Vernon Scannell*   145

A comment on happiness and fulfilment in three women's lives. Which words and phrases set the scene in the first three verses? Why is the third woman different from the other two?

They discuss their daydreams: what are the fantasies of the first two women? Why do they need to dream of such things? Which phrase sums up their dissatisfaction with their present lives? What is the dream of the third woman? Why is this a bleak kind of joke and what comment does it make about human happiness?

Pick out ideas and images to do with playing parts, a key theme in the poem.

▷ : Write your own dialogue in which three people, perhaps of different generations, disagree about the meaning of happiness.

Hay for the Horses   *Gary Snyder*   147

Snyder, employed as a labourer on a Californian farm, reflects on a conversation with an elderly farm-truck driver. What comment does this man make on his work? What general comment is made in the poem about unhappiness? Is there any hint of a solution?

The Road not Taken   *Robert Frost*   147

At the age of 38, Frost gave up being a successful New England farmer and teacher, and came to England 'to be poor and to write poetry'.

This poem is about the choices we make in life. He relates the decisions we all have to face, to a walk through a wood when we have to decide which path to follow. Which path does he choose in the poem? What is unusual about this choice? What do you understand by the last line? What are the advantages of using a metaphor to define an abstract idea like 'making choices'?

▷ : What difficult choices do you have in your own life in the next few years that might be shown as dividing paths like Frost's? You could set them out as a diagram, and then write about them.

Outside   *Anne Tibble*   148

An abandoned church makes Anne Tibble think about decaying religious beliefs. Outline the condition of this country church. What are the most important words in this description? Who were Belinda, Jane, Ivy and Tom? How would they have behaved towards the church?

Modern boys live in a very different world. What do they do to the church? Why? The boys do not steal from the building: why not? The poet calls them *those heirs of our violence*. What does this mean (think of what has happened during this century)?

What happens to the church as a result of the boys' vandalism? In the last two lines, the poet reaches some conclusions. What are these? What general theme emerges from the poem? Is the poet angry, sad or puzzled?

▷ : Your thoughts and observations as you explore an empty church, or sit in a service in one that is still active.

In a Country Church   *R. S. Thomas*   149

R. S. Thomas, himself a clergyman, writes about the experiences of religious doubt and faith.

Which are the important words in the first line? What is the *wind's song*? What did the kneeling man perhaps hope to hear? What two meanings does he give to the *unseen wings*? Which adjectives express his feelings of lack of faith in verse one?

What is the final result of his long prayer? With whom are the *dark crown of thorns* and *fruit of a man's body* connected? Which words express the restoration of religious hope and faith in the man at prayer in the church?

Photograph of Haymaker, 1890   *Molly Holden*   150

The poet is looking at an old photograph of a farm-worker cutting hay. One appeal of the photograph is the old-fashioned work. Another is the mower's costume. But more interesting is the idea that the photograph defeats time, as it shows the sunlight of a long-lost summer in the last century.

What does she find especially moving about the uncut flowers and grass in the picture? Compare with this passage from the 'Burial of the Dead' service in *The Book of Common Prayer*:

> Man that is born of woman hath but a short time to live, and is full of misery. He cometh up, and is cut down, like a flower; he fleeth as it were a shadow, and never continueth in one stay.

How do the flowers in the picture relate to human beings? The labourer's figure may also remind us of 'Old Father Time', cutting down all life before him with a scythe.

▷ : Study some old photographs, preferably from the nineteenth century. Write, as Molly Holden has done, about what you find curious and interesting about the remote scenes and figures.

Some Pictures of the Thirties   *Vernon Scannell*   150

Scannell is looking through a book of photographs of the 1930s, the decade in which he grew up. His own memories colour what he sees.

The first verse is about the book. What colour are the pictures? What image defines this colour? Which words describe the streets in the photographs? How does he tell us about working men's clothes of the time? What does he find so hard to grasp about the pictures?

The next two verses show what he adds to the book from his own memory, *the darkening archives of the skull*. What colours, sights and sounds does he recall? What, in his memory, was the chief quality of that time?

The fourth verse records the grimmer aspects of the Thirties, such as the marches of the unemployed (like the Jarrow Marchers, who walked from the North East to London in 1936). There were old soldiers on these marches; hence the references to medals, and *a long, long trail* (a popular soldiers' song of 1914–18).

Scannell then studies pictures of boxers. (He was a boxer himself.) Why do you think there were so few heavy-weights?

When he puts down the book and switches off the light, the pictures continue in his mind. What experiences, big and small, are recalled? What is he saying in the last sentence, do you think?

▷ : Look at some old photographs of the recent past, either in your family album or in a book, and try to recreate some of your own memories and experiences associated with the pictures.

Above Pate Valley   *Gary Snyder*   152

The poet is working as a labourer on a mountain road in California. Work stops for lunch, and Snyder describes the wild landscape around him.

In the grass he finds black flakes of stone. These are chippings from arrowheads made by Indian tribes thousands of years ago. He can suddenly imagine these long-vanished people and feels links with them. How does he see himself as different from them? What feeling is contained in the last line?

Dinosaurs   *Roy Fuller*   153

In a museum, the poet studies a dinosaur skeleton. There is an *opening of doors* in his mind. He becomes puzzled by the thought of dinosaurs dominating the earth's life, as they did for 65 million years, while man's whole history spans only two million. He cannot imagine our world, *this all-familiar sphere*, in the age of dinosaurs.

Thinking of their rise and fall makes him wonder about mankind's fate. It seems strange that man rules the earth now. What, does he suggest, might replace men? How might this come about?

Compare with William Stafford's *At the Bomb Testing Site*, (p. 37).

▷: Your own vision of earth in the age of dinosaurs.

During Wind and Rain   *Thomas Hardy*   153

The poem is based on Emma Hardy's description of her youth, in her autobiography, *Some Recollections*. After his wife's death in 1912, Hardy visited her birthplace, Plymouth, to explore the places she mentioned and to see the graves of her relatives.

Vivid scenes from the past life of the family are presented to us. What is the family doing in the first memory picture? What do you think Hardy's invented word *mooning* means?

In the second picture, the family is improving a large beautiful garden. In the third, they are breakfasting in this garden in summer. Tame birds eat from their hands. The sea is seen in the distance. In the last verse, the family is moving and their fine possessions are spread on the lawn, waiting for removal. Which picture do you find most striking?

The memory pictures – with their themes of happiness, harmony, and constructive activity – are optimistic. How do the refrains change the mood of each verse? What exactly is mentioned in each refrain? The most memorable is the last: what does the word *ploughs* suggest that rain and time are doing to the family names on the gravestones?

What does this poem have to say about the passing of time?

▷: Then and now: a set of similar images of a family's past and present.

Working Girls   *Carl Sandburg*   154

On an early morning city street, Sandburg watches crowds of women walking to work. Young and middle-aged move side by side.

What contrast does he make between the thoughts he imagines passing through the minds of young and older women? Does he admire one group more than the other? What consolation does the poem offer to our fears of growing older?

▷: Write, as a dialogue, the thoughts of two people of different generations who are next to each other at the same event (a wedding, a party, a school occasion, for example).

The Three O'clock Shift   *Wilfrid Gibson*   155
Gibson sympathizes with coal miners rising before dawn to begin their shift down the pit. As they pass his house, he is mostly aware of sounds. What are these? Why do they seem pitiful?

Labour Exchange   *Clifford Dyment*   156
The poet watches men waiting at the Labour Exchange, in the 1930s. They have come to draw the dole and to look for work.

Which adjectives are most forceful in describing the men? What telling details are given of their home life? What is the *blazing stadium*?

In the second verse, the clock is given the qualities of a human being. Who is this? Which phrases define the person's work and attitude to the men?

What point is made in the last two lines? What is the tone of this poet's comment on unemployment?

The Explosion   *Philip Larkin*   156
Larkin writes about a coal-mining disaster. The mine-shafts are set in the middle of pleasant countryside, which the miners delight in as they walk to first shift in the *freshened silence* of early morning. There is an underground explosion, in which many men are killed. At a memorial service for the men, their wives experience a vision of them in the after-life.

The poem is built around contrasts. How is the manner of the men set against the way one of them treats the lark's nest that he finds in the grass? How does the violence of the explosion contrast with the way it is felt on the surface? (Note the break in rhythm in verse five that marks the shock.) How is the final picture of the unbroken eggs set against the explosion underground?

▷: A newspaper account of the mining disaster, including reports from some of the local people involved.

When I heard the learn'd astronomer   *Walt Whitman*   157
Whitman attends a lecture on the stars by a famous astronomer. Unimpressed by the mathematical account of the universe, he goes outside to look in perfect silence at the splendour and mystery of the starlit skies.

The poem compares the scientific with the imaginative attitude to natural wonders.

Notice how the theme is reflected in the way that the jerky rhythm of the lists in the first four lines, moves to the smoother rhythm of the poem's conclusion. The plain, factual words of the opening, are set against richer, more evocative language of the last three lines. Pick out some of these.

See *Happiness* by Carl Sandburg, (p. 145).

▷: Your own thoughts on contemplating the starlit skies.

The Fox   *Robert Gittings*   158

The poem is based on an episode from *The Voyage of the Beagle* by the Victorian scientist, Charles Darwin (1809–1882), who first set down the theory of evolution.

During a visit to the island of San Pedro on his voyage into the South Atlantic in 1831–3, Darwin killed an unusual fox to study as part of his scientific work.

The first part of the poem sees the arrival of the ship, 'Beagle', through the eyes of the fox. What impression of the creature's behaviour is given? How is Darwin made to seem furtive and guilty? Which words and phrases express the poet's disapproval of Darwin's work? Gittings sees the killing as heartless. The fox has a right to its own life: it should not be used simply as a specimen in the elaboration of Darwin's theory.

What does the poet see as evolving from such a lack of feeling? Who are the *animals of science*? How does he link the fox story to the creation of the atomic bomb? What does he regret about thoughtful people, *the wise and brave*, in regard to scientific development?

Open Day at Porton   *Adrian Mitchell*   159

Porton Down in Wiltshire is a large British Government research station, where experiments in chemical and biological weapons are conducted.

The poet regards such work as dangerous, insane and immoral. He satirizes the research by inventing *liquid madness*, a new weapon. What examples does he give of the effect of the substance? Which bitter point is made by the sentence, *There is no damage to property*?

The second half of the poem makes fun of some of the arguments used to justify research into terrible new weapons. What are some of these? What is the effect of the phrase *responsible madness*?

▷ : There is an accident at the Research Station: write a story about this and its consequences.

Mrs. Middleditch   *William Plomer*   160

Worn down by age and the sorrows of widowhood, Mrs. Middleditch feels that life is empty and pointless. Which lines sum up these feelings?

What aspects of the supermarket does the poet criticize? Mrs. Middleditch talks to a younger woman there (verse eight). How do their ideas differ?

What vision comes to Mrs. Middleditch (verse twelve onwards) as she looks at the rich produce on the shelves? Which words and phrases are most forceful here?

She realizes that only *work* and *love* could help the misery of the poor in the Third World. She carries their sorrow within herself. If she tried to help them, she would be like the pelican that (according to legend) feeds its young from its own blood.

Besides telling the individual story of Mrs. Middleditch, what else is the poem saying?

Geography Lesson   *Zulfikar Ghose*   164
A poem about changing perspectives as you look out from an aeroplane climbing into the sky.

The poet watches from the window as his airliner takes off. He sees the pattern of the city below him. What conclusion does he draw from this?

At ten thousand feet, he can see a vast span of country. What does he now understand about the *logic of geography*?

At six miles, he can see the curvature of the Earth. What puzzles him now about human life? What do you think the poet is saying about us and our world?

Happiness   *Roy Fuller*   165
A contemporary comment on mankind's future. Fuller suddenly sees that his present life-style may be seen one day as part of a 'Golden Age' of peace and plenty. What are *benign routines*? Why mention *eggs* and *isolation in gardens*? What glimpse of the possible future does he give us? Who do you think the *crowding/visitors* might be?

▷: A story based on the future vision depicted in the poem, *or* your own hopes and fears about the future of mankind.

So that we build   *Martin Carter*   165
The poet observes the approach of a tropical storm in the West Indies. Which words convey the drama of this sudden change in the weather?

The mighty storm makes him think of Noah's flood in the *Old Testament* story. Which aspects of the story appeal to him? What does he hope will happen to our modern world? What would he like to happen after a new 'Great Flood'. Make a list of some of the aspects of contemporary life that the poet may be thinking of in his phrase, *floods of misery*?

IMAGININGS

From the Domain of Arnheim   *Edwin Morgan*   166
Two time travellers from an advanced civilization of the future, journey into the past to examine the lives of their remote human ancestors, struggling to survive during an Ice Age.

What do they see and hear during their visit? What event is being celebrated by the primitive people? How do the primitives sense the arrival of the invisible time travellers? What does the *sweating trumpeter* do to ward them off?

When the time travellers return home, their reaction to their experiences is unforseen. They don't value the specimens – rocks and seeds – they have brought back, but a quality they have seen in the prehistoric human beings. What is this?

The phrase, *Domain of Arnheim*, is borrowed from a story by the nineteenth century American writer, Edgar Allan Poe. Poe told of an immensely rich man, who uses his vast fortune to build a huge, fantastic, beautiful landscape garden. In one way the title of this poem is therefore a kind of joke: the landscape visited by the time travellers is grim and inhospitable, anything but beautiful, – redeemed only by the qualities of its inhabitants. Or it could be that the travellers live in too comfortable and protected a society, and so admire the Ice Age world as being adventurous and interesting.

▷: Supposing that time travel were possible – *either* write a story describing some of your adventures in time *or* discuss those periods, in past or future, which would be most curious to explore.

Limbo   *D. M. Thomas*   167

The poem is cast in the form of a letter by a spacecraft captain to his wife, Zoë. He writes of a moral decision he had to make when he discovers a stowaway on his ship during an interplanetary voyage.

How is the boy discovered? What is he like? What is his fate? Why is this? How does he react? How does the captain justify himself to his wife?

▷: *Either* the full story of this incident, telling what happened before and after the finding of the space stowaway.

Or write a dialogue between the captain and the stowaway.

A Dead Planet   *D. M. Thomas*   168

In the distant future, alien space explorers visit a nuclear-devastated Earth, where human life has become extinct. What hints are there of the appearance of these aliens? Which lines tell you about the nuclear war? Which phrases describe the desolate landscape?

So advanced is the aliens' science that they can take a fragment of human skull and recreate a living man from it. When the man comes to life again, where does he think he is? What does he think has happened to him? What does *his faith was not in vain* mean? What are the mood and meaning of the last four lines of the poem? (*Its true estate* means the nature and capability of the human being.)

▷: Tell the story from the point of view of the man, starting at the time of the Last War, and including his 'rebirth' and ultimate fate.

Missionary   *D. M. Thomas*   169

The opening lines are in imitation of T. S. Eliot's *Journey of the Magi*, which is about the mystery of Christ's birth:

A cold coming we had of it
Just the worst time of the year
For a journey, and such a long journey,
The ways deep and the weather sharp,
The very dead of winter. . .

How, in science fiction terms, are these points 'explained' in the poem: the Bethlehem star; the birth in the stable; Jesus' teaching about heaven; the crucifixion and ascension; the teachings of Christianity?

What, according to Thoorin, the alien Vardian, will happen in the distant future of the Earth? What happened to alien agents sent to other planets? How does this tie in with Christianity?

The Horses   *Edwin Muir*   172

Muir imagines a war that has caused the collapse of civilization. Only a few people in remote communities survive. One group lives on an island, like Muir's own native Orkneys. They see and hear signs of the war from a distance: what are these? What are their feelings about the catastrophe?

With machines now useless, they revert to a medieval way of life, *far past our fathers' land*. One evening, mysterious horses appear from nowhere, offering themselves for use and a new era begins.

The Biblical myths of the creation and the flood lie behind the poem. The war is like another flood; the coming of the horses like a second Genesis. Hints of these myths are given throughout the poem. The war is seven days long. How does this relate to Genesis? Men make a *covenant with silence*, just as God made a covenant with Noah and *every living creature*. Note also that the horses come *from their own Eden*.

Why has God destroyed civilization? What do machines seem to be doing to themselves in the first part of the poem? God gives the horses to men to recreate a *long-lost archaic companionship*. Why is man's contact with horses superior to his use of machines?

Examine the full stop and line-end pauses in the first section of the poem. How do they help to create the effect of silence in the post-war world? Pick out words and phrases which convey the magic and mystery of the horses.

▷: A story based on the experiences of one of the islanders in the poem.

GENERAL QUESTIONS

1. Some of these poems deal with personal matters; some with wider social issues. Choose one of each kind and write about them, making clear what you find impressive in their content or style.

2. How do these poets deal with one of these themes: happiness; work; time; science; the uneasy world of the late twentieth century?

3. What do you find curious, strange and interesting in the selection of science fiction poems?

GLOSSARY OF
TECHNICAL TERMS

Alliteration   a sequence of the same consonant sound at the beginning of words. It creates a particular effect by tying words together. Eg. *They sang their way to the siding-shed*, Wilfred Owen, *The Send-Off* (p. 20).

Ambiguity   a word or expression that carries more than one meaning. Eg. the titles *A Front*, Randall Jarrell (p. 34), or *Travelling through the Dark*, William Stafford (p. 56).

Antithesis   a clash of strongly contrasted words or phrases. Eg. *Marshals gilt and red/simple cemeteries; noble sacrifice/wooden crosses*, Siegfried Sassoon, *Great Men* (p. 16).

Archaism   old-fashioned or out-dated words used because of their association with the past, or to fit the metre of a poem. Eg. *unwontedly, no whit*, Edward Thomas, *Adlestrop* (p. 72); *'tis, ay, nought*, Walter de la Mare, *The Ghost* (p. 98).

Assonance   repetition of vowel sounds in a sequence of words that are placed together. Eg. *the sweet cheat gone*, Walter de la Mare, *The Ghost* (p. 98).

Autobiographical   concerned with memories of a person's own life. Eg. *Discord in Childhood*, D. H. Lawrence (p. 111), and *Carrickfergus*, Louis Macneice (p. 113), are autobiographical poems.

Colloquial   using the language of everyday, familiar speech. Eg. *shoved, slammed up, yells*, Carl Sandburg, *Buttons* (p. 12); *drop in, popped out*, Tony Harrison, *Long Distance* (p. 118).

Elegy   a poem about mourning or sadness, usually associated with death. Eg. *My Mother*, Claude McKay (p. 115); *Futility*, Wilfred Owen (p. 21).

Epigram   a very short, neatly-turned poem that ends with a clever or surprising thought. Eg. *On the Ridgeway*, Andrew Young (p. 86).

Imagery   an image uses words to create a picture which often stands for or suggests something else. Eg. *red and yellow buttons – blue and black buttons – are shoved/back and forth across the map*, Carl Sandburg, *Buttons (p. 12)*.
    Similes and **metaphors** are two different kinds of image.

Lyric   a short (or fairly short) poem that usually expresses the personal feelings and thoughts of the poet. The narrator may be the poet himself or an imaginary person, as in Philip Larkin's *Wedding-Wind*, (p. 95).
    A lyric often has the quality of a song or music.

Metaphor   a kind of image; something is compared to another indirectly, by suggestion. Eg. in *First Frost*, Andrei Voznesensky (p. 88), icy winter stands for or suggests human cruelty and sorrow. Or in *An Anniversary* Vernon Scannell (p. 94), the listlessness of the river reflects the sad mood of the poet.

An extended metaphor can involve a whole poem. Eg. *The Road not Taken*, Robert Frost (p. 147), where the road represents choice in life, and the poem explores the consequences of choice.

Metre   the rhythm of lines of poetry, based on the number of stressed syllables in each line. Eg. Siegfried Sassoon's *Suicide in the Trenches*, (p. 15) has four stressed and four unstressed syllables to a line; *In winter trenches, cowed and glum,/With crumps and lice and lack of rum.*

Narrative   story-telling in verse; the narrator is the story-teller. *Missionary*, D. M. Thomas (p. 169), *Mrs. Middleditch*, William Plomer (p. 160), and *Not to keep*, Robert Frost (p. 18), are narrative poems.

Onomatopoeia   an effect created by words that imitate sounds. Eg. 'moo' or 'pop'. In *Spring Offensive* Wilfred Owen, (p. 19) an onomatopoeic effect is used in the second verse to create a sleepy mood, with the repeated *z* and *ss* sounds – *breeze, murmurous, oozed, grass, glass.* Robert Browning's *Meeting at Night*, (p. 89), also includes many onomatopoeic effects; *tap, quick sharp scratch, spurt.*

Pathetic Fallacy   inanimate objects and landscapes are given human feelings and moods. Eg. *After a Romantic Day*, Thomas Hardy (p. 86), and the third verse of Wilfred Owen's *Spring Offensive*, (p. 19).

Phrase   a group of words that does not make up a full sentence.

Refrain   a line or group of lines, usually at the end of a verse, which is repeated during the poem, rather like a chorus. Eg. W. B. Yeats, *What then?* (p. 144);

> *'What then?' sang Plato's ghost. 'What then?'*

Or, *During Wind and Rain*, Thomas Hardy (p. 153);

> *Ah, no; the years O!*
> *Ah, no: the years, the years.*

Rhyme   exact sound echo, which can be used to give shape and force to the poet's thoughts, as in W. H. Auden's *Embassy* (p. 28) for example.

Sometimes a **Half Rhyme** can be used; this is a near but not exact rhyme or echo effect, which gives shape and control, without the bounciness of full rhyme.

See *Futility*, Wilfred Owen (p. 21) – *sun/sown, star/stir.*

The pattern of rhymes within a poem is called a **rhyme scheme**.

Eg. The first stanza of W. H. Auden's *Embassy* (p. 28), has an ABAB rhyme scheme;

As evening fell the day's oppression lifted:	A
Tall peaks came into focus: it had rained:	B
Across wide lawns and cultured flowers drifted	A
The conversation of the highly trained.	B

Or Philip Larkin's *The Trees* (p. 71), has an ABBA rhyme scheme:

The trees are coming into leaf	A
Like something almost being said:	B
The recent buds relax and spread.	B
Their greenness is a kind of grief.	A

Satire   attacking faults in people or society by mockery, and bitter laughter. *The Hero*, Siegfried Sassoon (p. 14), and *Open Day at Porton*, Adrian Mitchell (p. 159) are satirical poems.

Simile   a direct comparison in which one thing is likened to another; it usually begins with 'like' or 'as'. Eg. *flapping along the fire-step like a fish*, Siegfried Sassoon, *The Effect* (p. 15).

Stanza   is another name for a verse. Stanzas or verses are usually uniformly shaped. The verse pattern is made up of the number of lines, the rhythm of each line and the **rhyme scheme**.

Style   the way in which a writer expresses ideas. A writer's style may be studied by considering points like choice of words (diction), sentence structure, use of imagery, use of rhythm and sounds.

Symbol   a thing representing an idea. Eg. in Thomas Hardy's *Under the Waterfall* (p. 89), the glass symbolizes the unbroken love between Emma and Hardy. The tree in D. H. Lawrence's *Discord in Childhood* (p. 111) is a symbol of the aggression within the family.

Theme   the general idea suggested by a poem. Eg. a scientific attitude is the theme of Robert Gittings' *The Fox* (p. 158), and time and change are the themes of Thomas Hardy's *During Wind and Rain* (p. 153).

Tone   the mood of a poem. Eg. *Great Men*, Siegfried Sassoon (p. 16), is bitter and angry in tone, whilst *Always Marry an April Girl*, Ogden Nash (p. 88), is tender and lighthearted.

INDEX OF FIRST LINES

Acknowledgements

The editor and publisher are grateful for permission to use copyright material in this book.

Herbert Asquith: 'The Volunteer' from *Poems 1912–33*. Reprinted by permission of Sidgwick & Jackson Ltd.

W. H. Auden: 'Embassy', 'Epitaph on a Tyrant', 'Refugee Blues' and 'That night when joy began' from *Collected Poems*. Reprinted by permission of Faber & Faber Ltd.

John Betjeman: 'Devonshire Street W.1.', from *Collected Poems* (1970). Reprinted by permission of John Murray (Publishers) Ltd.

John Blight: 'Death of a Whale', from *A Beachcomber's Diary*. Reprinted by permission of Angus & Robertson (UK) Ltd.

Edward Kamau Brathwaite: Part I of 'Ancestors', from *Islands*. © OUP 1969. Reprinted by permission of Oxford University Press.

Gwendolyn Brooks: 'A Song in the Front Yard', from *The World of Gwendolyn Brooks*. Copyright 1945 by Gwendolyn Brooks Blakely. Reprinted by permission of Harper & Row, Publishers, Inc.

May Wedderburn Cannan: 'The Armistice'. Reprinted by permission of James C. Slater.

Martin Carter: 'So that we build', from *Poems of Succession* (1977). Reprinted by permission of New Beacon Books Ltd.

Charles Causley: 'What has happened to Lulu?', from *Collected Poems* (Macmillan, 1975). Reprinted by permission of David Higham Associates Ltd.

Frances Cornford: 'Childhood', from *Collected Poems*. First published by the Cresset Press 1954. Reprinted by permission of the Hutchinson Publishing Group Ltd.

Bruce Dawe: 'Home-Coming', from *Sometimes Gladness: Collected Poems 1954–1982*. Reprinted by permission of Longman Cheshire Pty. Limited.

Walter de la Mare: 'The Ghost'. Reprinted by permission of The Literary Trustees of Walter de la Mare and The Society of Authors as their representative.

Keith Douglas: 'Vergissmeinnicht', from *The Complete Poems of Keith Douglas*, ed. Desmond Graham (1978). © Marie J. Douglas 1978. Reprinted by permission of Oxford University Press.

Douglas Dunn: 'St. Kilda's Parliament', from *War Blinded* (Faber, 1981). Reprinted by permission of Faber & Faber Ltd.

Clifford Dyment: 'The Son' from *Collected Poems*. Reprinted by permission of J. M. Dent & Sons Ltd., Publishers. 'Labour Exchange' was first published in *New Writing: New Series 2* (Hogarth, 1939) and is reprinted by permission of Miss Irene Dyment.

Robert Frost: 'Not to keep', 'Reluctance' and 'The Road not Taken', from *The Poetry of Robert Frost*, edited by Edward Connery Lathem. Reprinted by permission of the Estate of Robert Frost and Jonathan Cape Ltd.

Roy Fuller: 'Dinosaurs' and 'Happiness', from *Tiny Tears* (André Deutsch). Reprinted by permission of the author.

Karen Gershon: 'I was not there', from *Selected Poems* (Gollancz). Reprinted by permission of the author.

Zulfikar Ghose: 'Geography Lesson', from *Jets of Orange* (1967). Reprinted by permission of Macmillan, London and Basingstoke.

Wilfrid Gibson: 'Girl's Song', from *Collected Poems*; 'The Three O'clock Shift', from *The Golden Room and Other Poems*. Reprinted by permission of Mr Michael Gibson and of Macmillan, London and Basingstoke.

Robert Gittings: 'The Fox', from *Collected Poems* (1976). Reprinted by permission of Heinemann Educational Books.

Ivor Gurney: 'The Target', from *War's Embers*. Reprinted by permission of Sidgwick & Jackson Ltd.

Tony Harrison: 'Long Distance', from *Continuous* (1982). Reprinted by permission of the author and Rex Collings Ltd.

Seamus Heaney: 'Digging', from *Death of a Naturalist* (1966). Reprinted by permission of Faber & Faber Ltd.

Adrian Henri: Parts 1, 2 and 3 from *Autobiography* (Cape). Copyright © 1971 by Adrian Henri. Reprinted by permission of Deborah Rogers Ltd.

Molly Holden: 'Photograph of Haymaker, 1890' and 'Teens', from *To Make Me Grieve* (1968). Reprinted by permission of the author's Literary Estate and Chatto & Windus Ltd.

Graham Hough: 'Death in the Village', from *Legends and Pastorals* (1961). Reprinted by permission of Gerald Duckworth & Co., Ltd.

Ted Hughes: 'To Paint a Water Lily', from *Lupercal*; 'Sheep 1', 'Spring Nature Notes 1' and 'The Stag', from *Season Songs*; 'The Jaguar', from *The Hawk in the Rain*. Reprinted by permission of Faber & Faber Ltd.

Randall Jarrell: 'A Front', from *The Complete Poems of Randall Jarrell*. Reprinted by permission of Faber & Faber Ltd.

Brian Jones: 'For Cathy, on going to turn out her light' and 'Gardening Sunday', from *For Mad Mary*. Reprinted by permission of London Magazine Editions.

Philip Larkin: 'Cut Grass', 'The Explosion' and 'The Trees', from *High Windows*; 'Love Songs in Age' and 'MCMXIV', from *The Whitsun Weddings*. Reprinted by permission of Faber & Faber Ltd. 'Wedding-Wind' and 'At Grass' from *The Less Deceived*. Reprinted by permission of The Marvell Press.

D. H. Lawrence: 'A Winter's Tale', 'Discord in Childhood', and 'Green' from *The Complete Poems* (Heinemann, 1976). Reprinted by permission of the Estate of Mrs. Frieda Lawrence Ravagli and Laurence Pollinger Ltd.

Denise Levertov: 'What were they like?', from *The Sorrow Dance* (1968). Reprinted by permission of Laurence Pollinger Ltd.

Louis MacNeice: 'Carrickfergus' and 'The Cyclist', from *The Collected Poems of Louis MacNeice*. Reprinted by permission of Faber & Faber Ltd.

Claude McKay: 'My Mother', from *The Selected Poems of Claude McKay*. Copyright 1981 and reprinted with the permission of Twayne Publishers, a division of G. K. Hall & Co., Boston.

Adrian Mitchell: 'Open Day at Porton', from *Ride the Nightmare*. Reprinted by permission of Jonathan Cape Ltd., on behalf of the author.

Ruth Comfort Mitchell: 'He went for a soldier', from *Poems of the Great War*.

Edwin Morgan: 'From the Domain of Arnheim' and 'Trio'. Copyright the author. Reprinted by permission.

Andrew Motion: 'Anne Frank Huis', from *Secret Narratives*. Reprinted by permission of The Salamander Press Edinburgh Limited.

Edwin Muir: 'Childhood', 'The Horses' and 'The Interrogation', from *The Collected Poems of Edwin Muir*. Reprinted by permission of Faber & Faber Ltd.

Ogden Nash: 'Always Marry an April Girl', from *I Wouldn't Have Missed It* (1983). Reprinted by permission of André Deutsch.

Wilfred Owen: 'Futility', 'Spring Offensive' and 'The Send-Off', from *The Complete Poems and Fragments*, ed. Jon Stallworthy, 1983. Reprinted by permission of the author's Literary Estate and Chatto & Windus Ltd.

Sylvia Plath: 'Morning Song', from *Ariel* (Faber). Copyright Ted Hughes 1965. Reprinted by permission of Olwyn Hughes.

William Plomer: 'Mrs. Middleditch', from *Taste and Remember*. Reprinted by permission of Jonathan Cape Ltd., on behalf of the Estate of William Plomer.

Peter Porter: 'Your Attention Please', from *Collected Poems*. © Peter Porter 1983. Reprinted by permission of Oxford University Press.

Alfred Purdy: 'Trees at the Arctic Circle', from *North of Summer* (1967). Used by permission of The Canadian Publishers, McClelland and Stewart Limited, Toronto.

John Crowe Ransom: 'Blue Girls' and 'Janet Waking', from *Selected Poems* (Eyre & Spottiswoode, 1970). Reprinted by permission of Laurence Pollinger Ltd.

Theodore Roethke: 'The Meadow Mouse', from *The Collected Poems of Theodore Roethke*. Reprinted by permission of Faber & Faber Ltd.

Siegfried Sassoon: 'Great Men', 'Suicide in the Trenches', 'The Effect' and 'The Hero', from *War Poems* (Faber, 1983). Reprinted by permission of George Sassoon.

Carl Sandburg: 'Buttons', 'Happiness' and 'Working Girls', from *Chicago Poems*. Reprinted by permission of Harcourt Brace Jovanovich, Inc.

Vernon Scannell: 'Picnic on the Lawn' from *Winter Man*. Reprinted by permission of the author and Allison & Busby Ltd. 'War Cemetery, Ranville', 'An Anniversary', 'Our Pale Daughters' and 'Where shall we go?', from *New and Collected Poems, 1950–1980*; 'The Bombing of the Café de Paris, 1941' and 'Some Pictures of the Thirties', from *Winterlude*. Reprinted by permission of Robson Books.

E. J. Scovell: 'Days drawing in'. Reprinted by permission of the author. 'To an Infant Grandchild', from *The Space Between* (1982). Reprinted by permission of Martin Secker & Warburg Ltd.

Louis Simpson: 'The Battle'. Reprinted by permission of the author.

Gary Snyder: 'Above Pate Valley' and 'Hay for the Horses'. Reprinted by permission of the author.

Stephen Spender: 'My parents kept me from children who were rough' from *Collected Poems*. Reprinted by permission of Faber & Faber Ltd.

William Stafford: 'At the Bomb Testing Site' and 'Travelling through the Dark' from *Stories That Could Be True: New and Collected Poems*. Copyright © 1960 by William Stafford. Reprinted by permission of Harper & Row, Publishers, Inc.

Edward Storey: 'On Platform 5' from *A Man in Winter*. Reprinted by permission of the author.

D. M. Thomas: 'A Dead Planet', 'Limbo' and 'Missionary'. Reprinted by permission of the author.

Dylan Thomas: 'Fern Hill' from *The Poems* (J. M. Dent). Reprinted by permission of David Higham Associates Ltd.

R. S. Thomas: 'The Evacuee' and 'Children's Song' from *Songs At the Year's Turning*; 'In a Country Church' from *Selected Poems*. Reprinted by permission of Granada Publishing Limited. 'Good' from *Laboratories of the Spirit*. Reprinted by permission of Macmillan, London and Basingstoke.

Anne Tibble: 'Outside'. Copyright the Estate of Anne Tibble.

John Tripp: 'Conditions of Pain' and 'Dismissal', from *Collected Poems 1958–78*. Reprinted by permission of Christopher Davies Ltd.

Andrei Voznesensky: 'First Frost' from *Antiworlds and the Fifth Ace*. © 1966 by Basic Books, Inc., Publishers. Reprinted by permission of the publishers.

Kath Walker: 'Municipal Gum', from *My People*. Reprinted by permission of Jacaranda Wiley Ltd.

Andrew Waterman: 'Suburban Eden', from *From the Other Country*. Reprinted by permission of Carcanet Press. 'A Butterfly', from *Living Room*. Reprinted by permission of The Marvell Press.

Arthur Graeme West: 'The Night Patrol', from *Diary of a Dead Officer*. Reprinted by permission of George Allen & Unwin (Publishers) Ltd.

Richard Wilbur: 'He was', from *Poems 1943–56*. Reprinted by permission of Faber & Faber Ltd.

Judith Wright: 'To a Mare', from *Collected Poems 1942–1970* (Angus & Robertson Pty., 1971).

W. B. Yeats: 'What then?', from *The Collected Poems of W. B. Yeats*. Reprinted by permission of A. P. Watt Ltd., on behalf of Michael Yeats and Macmillan London, Ltd.

Andrew Young: 'On the Ridgeway', from *Complete Poems*. Reprinted by permission of Martin Secker & Warburg Ltd.

Every effort has been made to trace and contact copyright holders. We apologize for any errors or omissions in the above list and would be grateful to be notified of any corrections that should be incorporated in any future editions of this volume.

The publisher would like to thank the following for permission to reproduce photographs:

Bruce Coleman/Jane Burton, p. 55; Richard and Sally Greenhill, pp. 84 (top), 106 (top left), 107 (top); Geoff Howard, pp. 84 (bottom), 85, 107 (bottom); Imperial War Museum, pp. 8, 9; Natural History Photographic Agency/Adrian Davies, p. 54; Network/Barry Lewis, p. 106 (top right); Science Photo Library/Dr. Fred Espenak, pp. 142–3; John Twinning, p. 106 (bottom).